a THAMES
Moment

Gordon Cope

RMB
Victoria Vancouver Calgary

Rocky Mountain Books
www.rmbooks.com

Library and Archives Canada Cataloguing in Publication

Cope, Gordon, 1955-
A Thames moment / Gordon Cope.

Issued also in electronic format.
ISBN 978-1-897522-99-8

1. Cope, Gordon, 1955- —Travel—England—Henley-on-Thames.
2. Henley-on-Thames (England)—Description and travel.
3. Henley-on-Thames (England)—Biography.
I. Title.

DA690.H5C67 2010   914.25'79   C2010-902808-2

Front cover photo: *Beautiful river and yellow boat* by Natallia Yaumenenka

Printed in Canada

Rocky Mountain Books acknowledges the financial support for its publishing
program from the Government of Canada through the Canada Book Fund (CBF),
Canada Council for the Arts, and the province of British Columbia through
the British Columbia Arts Council and the Book Publishing Tax Credit.

Canada Council
for the Arts

Conseil des Arts
du Canada

BRITISH COLUMBIA
ARTS COUNCIL

The interior pages of this book have been produced on 100% post-consumer
recycled paper, processed chlorine free and printed with vegetable-based inks.

Mixed Sources
FSC

This book is dedicated in loving memory of Teddy Selwyn.

Author's Note

I have made very little effort to verify geographical and historical facts within this book and therefore advise the reader not to do anything rash, like wagering a bet on the contents. I do affirm that all embarrassing events herein occurred to the author. Some of the people mentioned in this book are real, the rest I made up. Any resemblance of fictional characters to real human beings is purely coincidental, and anyone who thinks they recognize themselves may be suffering from narcissism and should talk to their mirror.

CONTENTS

Prologue

I never wanted to come back to England. I've been here before, and I've seen what it can do to you.

My wife, Linda, and I were once given the opportunity to reside in London. Linda is an information technology analyst, an expert in the field of multi-currency accounting, and her company badly needed someone to open an office in London to service their European clientele. We jumped at the chance—we had always loved visiting the Capital, and living there would be a dream come true.

Based upon previous visits, we already knew where we wanted to live—South Kensington. Years ago, we had wandered the streets near Hyde Park, gazing in envy at row after row of white-columned Georgian mansions. In my febrile imagination, the neighbourhood invoked a crusty social world of Gilbert and Sullivan, Lady Diana, and the Beatles.

Through an estate agent, we found a wonderful apartment in Stanhope Gardens. Our landlord was in fact descended from the original Earl of Stanhope; Wills resembled a younger version of Sting and favoured buckskin jackets. He had decorated the apartment with a mixture of nineteenth-century prints, gold-flecked mantelpiece mirrors, and a CD jukebox filled with Lou Reed albums. An immense bay window in the living room looked out over the immaculate gardens across the street. The bay had been equipped with a dining-room set, just perfect for waving to the tourists as we drank afternoon tea in white gloves.

Living in Kensington gave us the opportunity to sample many of the delights that London had to offer. Every Saturday we went for a jog in Hyde Park and then took the Piccadilly Line into the

West End for a musical matinee followed by a glass of champagne in the patio of Palais du Jardin on Long Acre Road. Sundays were spent with the *Times*, reading about the latest MI6 traitor, royal family adultery, and dot-com miracle.

Unfortunately, our infatuation with London quickly uninfatuated. It wasn't any one thing in particular, but like porcupines making love, a combination of a thousand tiny pricks. The first was the disappointment of dining out. After several months of being bushwhacked by surly waiters, recipe-challenged kitchen staff, and *maitre d*'s so avaricious as to make a loan shark blush, London restaurants began to lose their lustre. In fact, if we were able to eat without suffering verbal abuse or personal bankruptcy we considered the evening a success.

But our biggest gripe was the sheer nastiness of London's inhabitants. We met snobs who viewed us as provincial colonials, social climbers who applied the kiss-up, kick-down rule of etiquette, and unfriendly neighbours. Late one Saturday night, I was out walking and happened to spot a co-resident of our row house named, ironically enough, Florence Nightingale. She was coming out of the Gloucester Road tube station just as I was passing, and I made the heinous error of saying hello. She shrank back, no doubt certain that this was a prelude to ravishment in front of the adjacent KFC. Granted, she had the better part of a quart of gin under her belt, but in all the time she had lived directly above us, Florence had never taken the time to even ascertain my identity.

When our two-year stint in London was over, we were out of there faster than a bishop in a bordello raid. But when we returned to Canada, no matter how passionately we whined, our friends could hardly believe us: "Merry Olde England is such a wonderful place to visit—surely it must be even better to live there!" they all said.

Perhaps London is an aberration from the British tradition of a warm, welcome society, but I was unconvinced and vowed never to return. Five years later, however, a client located just west of London was in dire need of Linda's help and offered her a one-year contract that was too generous to refuse. Once again, we found ourselves packing our bags, updating our work permits, and relocating to the land of scones and bangers-and-mash.

Drat.

1

AUGUST

In Search of Toffs and Twits

Ah, Reading—city of magic.

Linda and I are on the expressway that rings the city's downtown shopping district. We have been at a dead stop now for about twenty minutes, which gives us ample opportunity to admire the way the dark brown exterior of our rented Rover absorbs the August sun. On the plus side, this also gives me a chance to pull out a tourist guide and read about our new home. The annual Reading Festival of contemporary music is on today, which goes a long way toward explaining the military fatigues, facial metallica, and skullhead tattoos we've been seeing since our arrival—and that's just on the girls. We are passed by a strolling troupe of buskers playing plastic recorders. I tempt them with a handful of coins, but they refuse to cross between my bumper and the car in front. I must say, for entertainers, they really don't have much sense of fun.

The traffic jam finally eases, and we are able to advance to our hotel. Even though it is 3 PM, our room is not quite ready; the reception clerk recommends we go for a stroll through the centre of Reading, which has been renovated into a pedestrian mall. This proves to be an illuminating suggestion; the street is lined with quaint Victorian buildings, their façades of molded terra cotta frescoes and finely carved sandstone lintels all cleverly concealed by billboards for cellphone retailers and fast-food outlets. We reach the entrance to the Arcade, a sparkly new indoor mall specifically designed to reinvigorate the downtown core. It consists of a quarter-mile or so of emporiums where the good folks of Reading can buy their Nike shoes, Nokia phones, and FCUK jeans, all the while protected from the harmful effects of English air. It is also an excellent place to observe the locals in their native habitat. I stop to marvel at the thighs on a woman eating an ice cream sundae in the food court. Imagine if you will, a Volkswagen Beetle crammed into pink Lycra tights, and you'll pretty much have the right visual.

We return to the hotel, where the clerk announces it is safe to take up residence. The décor in our room has an African theme; it resembles a mud hut. The walls, curtains, and bedspread are decorated in beige, ecru, and several variations of bentonite. For relief, I stare out the bay window. To the north is a panoramic view of the gasworks and to the south, terrace estate homes roll into the distance in grey waves of brick. I pick up a welcome brochure that has been left upon the bureau. "Modern Reading is a revelation to most people," proclaims the title page. Tragically, I can't agree more. Linda cranks the bay window open; the breeze has shifted and the gentle aroma of a hide-rendering plant drifts into our room.

"It says here that suicide is Reading's favourite pastime," I note.

"I don't doubt it," says Linda. "We should find a place in another town."

I look up from the brochure. "Like where?"

"How about Henley-on-Thames?"

Located a little under sixteen kilometres northeast of Reading, Henley-on-Thames isn't one of those places that top the list of most well-known British tourist attractions. It is promoted as "a quaint Thames enclave," best known for its annual rowing regatta and as a hub for "caviar eating, champagne swilling, and antics."

But when we ask our British friends about that town, the response is unanimous.

"Full of toffs," says Zoe.

"Inbred twits," asserts Brendan.

Well, in my book, any town that's renowned for its champagne swilling beats Reading any day. Grabbing the car keys, we head out in search of Toffs and Twits.

After an hour of dodging faux Rasta kids, we finally clear the edge of Reading. Almost immediately, the grey terrace homes give way to idyllic English landscape. To the right, the River Thames is a distant, sinuous flash of crystal and silver. To the left, gentle mounds of emerald pasture rise to the horizon. Above, white clouds dawdle across a pastel blue sky. It's as though Reading never existed, which, I suspect, is a wish a lot of people make.

After a fifteen-minute drive, we pass a sign marking Henley's official boundary. As we enter the town from the south, we encounter a boring procession of red-brick terrace homes, petrol stations, building supply stores, and dry cleaners. On the plus side, we've been here almost three minutes and haven't spotted a single hippie. I park the car in a municipal lot and we set out to explore the centre of town. The Market Place is picturesque and charming, with a rather imposing town hall at one end. I am immediately struck by the fact that the square is free of the souvenir stores so favoured by Stratford-upon-Avon, where Ye Witches Brew Kitchen Shoppe and rubber Hamlet skulls abound. Apparently, Henley hasn't gone in for that, although I'm not quite sure what kind of mementoes might be engendered by alcoholic excess during a boat race.

We walk down to a pub by the bridge, the Angel. I order two pints of bitter and join Linda at a wooden picnic table on the patio adjacent to the water. The outdoor area is filled with cyclists in orange shorts and girls in tank tops and silver nose rings. A trio of large lads is laughing loudly enough to drown out the ten-tonne lorries rolling across the bridge above us. We ignore all this and stare out at the vista. Along the far bank of the river, weeping willows dangle languidly over slender rushes. The sun is beaming down against the forest-covered hills in the distance. Rowers, their backs erect, scull under the bridge. An elderly man in a blue blazer and straw boater hat putters upstream in an antique wooden boat. It's as if every cliché of every English countryside landscape has been plopped down in one place.

"This is where we're going to live," says Linda.

"How will you get to work in Reading?"

"We'll lease a car."

"What will I do here?"

"You can write a book."

"About what?"

A tall man comes goose-stepping across the bridge. He is about fifty, with a big handlebar moustache, green beret, and a long golf umbrella cocked over his right shoulder. When he reaches the end of the bridge, he marches out into the centre of the road, tucks the golf umbrella under the crook of his left arm, and smartly salutes the church tower.

"You'll find something," says Linda.

The next morning, I return to Henley, park the car in the large lot adjacent to the train station, and head toward the centre of town. Christ Church stands at the head of Station Road; the handsome hexagonal tower rises some twenty-four metres, capped by a cock's weather vane and fronted by a large clock. The church sits adjacent to a baptistery, wedding chapel, funeral parlour, and tombstone retailer—kind of a one-stop shop to Eternity. These English are damned efficient when it comes to metaphysics.

Farther north, Reading Road turns into Duke Street for no discernible reason. The buildings along this stretch of road are a monotonous series of two-storey brick edifices, whose appearance has been improved, if anything, by the addition of garish plywood signage, including an advertisement for a Chinese buffet announcing "Eat as Much as You Like," which, judging from the look of it, is more of a warning than an invitation.

I continue on to the Market Place, where I hope to spot some realty offices. The square is lined with the usual collection of banks and video chain stores, although there are also some one-offs, including a butcher and a men's clothing shop. A sign in the window of the clothing store promises "The finest in British fashion." If you ever want to make a Frenchman laugh until he squirts Pernod out his nose, mention Britain and fashion in the same sentence. This is the same country in which the city of London—in a move that would have been deeply ironic in any other country—decided to locate their new fashion museum in a factory that had once manufactured garbage bins.

The road north of the town hall is lined with a dreary stretch of Dickensian terrace homes, so I turn and retrace my steps back through Market Place to Hart Street. On my left is the Catherine Wheel pub, named after St. Catherine, an early Christian convert who annoyed the Roman emperor so much with her prattling that he chopped off her head and then tied the rest of her to a torture wheel in case she didn't get the point. The wheel spun round and round, throwing off sparks until it finally burst asunder and the body flew off toward Mount Sinai. I haven't a clue why anyone in Henley would name a pub after her, but my estimation of the town rises two notches.

The rest of Hart Street's architecture is pleasantly more varied than Duke Street, with styles ranging from Tyrolean Alps to Oxfordshire Gothic. One thing that disappoints me is the lack of allusions to George Orwell. Although the man who would grow up to write *Animal Farm* and *Nineteen Eighty-Four* wasn't born in

Henley, the former Eric Blair certainly spent enough of his formative years here for the town to make a credible claim on him as one of their own. Yet, I haven't spotted a single Big Brother TV Shop or Piggie's Trough. This town's got a serious case of good taste.

I finally spy a realty office near the end of Hart Street. The agent is a young man in his early twenties with spiky blond hair, black suit, and fluorescent purple tie. I pry him reluctantly away from a pornographic Web site to view some lettings near the centre of town.

My taste in homes is relatively modest. My only prerequisites are that it be within staggering distance of the nearest pub and has never served as a baboon sanctuary. Linda is more specific. She has furnished me with a list of twenty requirements and strict instructions not to deviate. Like most of my gender, I understand the consequences of disobeying.

The first home we look at is only a few metres from the Thames, but the kitchen is tricked out in avocado green appliances and the carpet features an orange, red, and green pattern. There is nothing on Linda's list prohibiting a carpet that induces epilepsy in direct sunlight, but I make a judgment call. The next stop is a Victorian terrace home. The exterior has been renovated to show off the authentic brick façade, but the rooms are so tiny that I envision sleeping with our feet hanging out the bedroom window. Since Linda's feet are already notoriously cold, I scratch this off the list as well.

I am about to give up for the day when I spot a second agency. Taped to their window is an ad for a home located on the waterfront. The townhouse is part of a small development adjacent to a marina and is clad in red brick, white wooden trim, and grey slate roofing. It even has a name: Boathouse Reach. It looks rather charming. The monthly rent is several hundred pounds out of our budget, but the thought of living directly adjacent to the river fills me with romantic visions. Sue the realtor, a petite, animated woman in a brown suit, agrees to arrange a showing that evening. I head back to Reading feeling, for the first time, a glimmer of hope.

After dinner, Linda and I drive back to Henley and meet Sue at Boathouse Reach. She opens the door and we walk through to the dining room overlooking the river. The interior of the home is done up in rather drab ivory walls and dark green carpet, and I am already considering ways to politely end the inspection when we come to the rear balcony and are confronted with an absolutely gorgeous view. Directly in front of us, tiny rowboats painted in yellow, blue, and red bob in their moorings. Across the river, tall columnar aspens sway in the breeze and, in the distance, the Chiltern Hills rise in oak-covered glory.

"We'll take it," says Linda.

Sue holds up a finger. "There is just one further requirement; you need to be vetted by the landlord." She dials her cellphone and makes a short call. "He'll meet us at the office."

We walk back toward town. Linda and Sue are engaged in an animated conversation regarding kitchen appliances, furnishings, and other non-essentials. I, on the other hand, am worried about meeting the landlord. Renting a home in England can be a nightmare, with endless delays. I envision a country squire in a tweed jacket and hairy eyebrows pounding back a succession of gin and tonics as he gives us the once-over. Is this going to be our first encounter with one of the Henley Toffs that Zoe had warned us about? I try to comport myself as something more presentable than an ink-stained wretch.

When we arrive at the office, Andy is waiting for us. He is perhaps seventy, with snow-white hair, large ears twisted by countless rugby scrums, and a face burned deep brown by a lifetime messing about on boats; I can't think of anyone who looks less like a Toff. I stick out my hand and he crushes it in a vicelike grip. His eyes, ice blue, stare at me for several seconds. "Where you from?" he finally asks.

"Canada."

"Ah." I get the distinct impression he is relieved I am not from Mars, or worse, the United States.

"When do you want to move in?"

"Monday, if that's all right."

"Fine by me." He calls over his shoulder as he turns to the door. "See you on Monday."

Linda has to work on Monday, so I drive to Henley to do the honours. At the appointed hour, Sue meets me at the house and formally hands over the keys. I enter and open the foyer closet to hang up my coat; inside, a large square metal box is chuffing and bubbling in a manner that indicates either acute indigestion or internal combustion, neither of which I particularly welcome in a receptacle for coats. Attached to the device is a bright red label warning one not to twiddle with the knobs unless death by scalding is one's hobby. I quickly close the door and continue my inspection.

The kitchen has been laid out according to classic British ergonomics, which means you can't open the cupboard doors without splitting your skull. The freezer portion of the fridge sports enough ice to build a snowman, and the oven interior is covered in an impressive coat of dark brown grease.

I go upstairs to the living room. The view from the balcony is just as magnificent as the main floor, but I now have the leisure to observe that the chairs and couches are covered in the same red, green, and yellow geometrical swirls seen when someone punches you smartly in the eye. A chaise lounge lurking in the corner wouldn't look out of place with Mae West in feather boas draped over it.

I retreat to the main bedroom on the top floor. Clinging to the side of the vanity by the window is a black blob that I first mistake for a false eyelash, but discover is a very large spider when I try to peel it off. I redeploy to the kitchen to fetch an oven mitt and spatula and adroitly detach the arachnid and fling it toward the window in a manner that would have been highly effective had the window actually been open. Fortunately, a spatula is also handy for flailing, and I reduce the spider to a carpet stain that is hardly noticeable from three metres.

Such exertion, of course, is thirsty work, but the previous tenants have neglected to leave so much as a can of lager in the house. A quick scan of the fridge and cupboards reveals nothing more than a jar of mustard (full) and a box of mouse poison (half-empty). I conclude this is insufficient to make dinner, and since I am in charge of cooking a meal this evening, I decide it is time to go shopping. I grab my coat and wallet and head for the grocery store.

As I step out the door, I spot a woman standing with her back to me, peering around the corner of the adjacent building. She has a small dog on a leash. The woman is perhaps fifty, with a sharp, beaklike nose and a dye job that started out as Tuscany Auburn but now looks more like Toyota Sunburn. The dog is a Yorkshire terrier cross, white with black markings. I step quietly outside then slam the door as loudly as possible.

The woman spins around so fast that she jerks her dog almost clear of the ground. Rather than being embarrassed, however, she bursts into a brilliant smile.

"Hello this is Princess and I'm Edwina and we live just around the corner we were just on my way to visit your neighbour Meg who's feeling poorly but who can blame her what with her husband Norris running off with his dentist to some nude beach in Ibiza and I always told her there was something funny about him but no he was so kind and gentle not like her first husband Dennis

18

who would chase anything in skirts and if you ever saw the rector's wife you'd know I mean *anything* but what can one do honestly?"

She finally stops for breath and blinks both her eyes slowly. "And what's your name?"

I must say, up to this point, I had feared that I might be dealing with an example of the Henley Inbred Twit, but I am so relieved by Edwina's effusive nosiness that I break into a broad smile. I have pursued many professions during my lifetime, including geologist, dynamite courier, and bowling lane jockey, but by far the most rewarding job I have ever had is that of journalist. Not only does it require a minimum of physical effort, but you can also gratify any ingrained nosiness and get paid, to boot. For most people, gossips are about as welcome as a dose of clap at the nunnery, but for a journalist, they're like manna sent by a benevolent, higher authority. I introduce myself and explain that my wife and I have just moved from Canada.

"Canada!" she effuses as the torrent begins anew. "My youngest nephew has been living in Edmonton he got a job there after graduating from Oxford first in his class we're so proud he's engaged to a wonderful girl from there apparently her father has a large household fixtures store and they call him the 'king of doorknobs' *hah* if you can believe it what some colonials…" She once again blinks both eyes slowly. "And what brings you here from Canada?"

I lean over to give Princess a pat and she licks my hand. "To convalesce. I just had a brain tumour removed."

"Oh, that's ghastly!" She leans forward, hopefully. "Cancerous?"

"No, thank God. But it was the size of an apple. They had to saw off the top of my skull and put in a hinge." I lean forward to show her my pate. "They did a great job—you can't even see the scar."

Edwina can barely conceal her delight. Tugging on Princess's leash, she bids adieu and scurries off to tell Meg. As I walk to the grocery store, I am filled with the warm glow I get when I do my civic duty.

The grocery store that dominates the centre of Henley-on-Thames belongs to the Waitrose chain. Unlike supermarkets in France, where you are just as likely to find toothpaste mixed in with the bacon, grocery stores in Britain have a certain predictability about them that is a testament to the solid, no-nonsense society that flourishes on this majestic isle; the vegetable section is on one side, dairy and meats on the other, and row after row of other tasteless stuff in the middle. Palatability is not an option.

This perception lasts as long as it takes me to read the label on a jar of Samoan Islands BBQ Sauce. I'm used to reading cooking suggestions like, "Tastes great with ribs!" so I am somewhat surprised to see that it says, "Suitable for vegetarians." I assume they must have a different flavour for missionaries, but I don't see it on the shelf. I put the jar carefully back, wipe my hands on my trousers, and retreat to the fresh vegetables.

I spot a young clerk throwing cabbage heads with furious agility into a display bin.

"Excuse me; do you know where I can find the red onions?" I ask.

The clerk gives me a look as if sizing up if there's room for one more head in the bin. "No red onions today."

I decide to have a gander for myself and, within about a minute, discover a large tub of red onions in the organic section. Taking one, I walk back to the clerk, waving it in his face. "You said there were no red onions."

"That's *organic* red onions. You didn't ask for them."

The next time I'm looking for a can of pickled herring, I'll remember to specify the left-handed variety, just for the sake of expediency.

That night, I cook a traditional English meal for Linda: bangers and mash. The dish consists of slowly roasted sausages served with creamy mashed potatoes and smothered with fresh onion gravy. As we gaze out onto the river from our dining room, we toast our new home with a glass of French Médoc. It is such a romantic evening, and the wine is so good, that we opt for a second bottle and soon abandon the dining room to check out the romantic view from the upstairs bedroom. Maybe that's why they say that red wine is so good for the heart.

Our first morning in Boathouse Reach dawns very early, with the light of the sun flooding in through the floor-to-ceiling windows in the master bedroom. I get up and gaze out onto a scene of transcendental beauty. Before me, a mist rises from the glasslike water and shrouds the Thames in a blanket of white. A lone sculler cuts through the water, his rhythmic strokes startling a swan near the shore. The bird splashes along the water then slowly gains the air, cutting along the boundary of the mist and clear sky. I stare out at this tranquil, almost ethereal scene, and one thought stands foremost in my mind: I'd better buy some curtains before they arrest me. For whatever reason, nobody has bothered to put up any sheers along the bottom of the window, and I am making a decidedly indecent show to a woman walking a greyhound through the marina below. That's the sort of thing that can get the neighbours talking, you know, and not in a complimentary way.

After breakfast, Linda departs for work, leaving me with a long list of chores. I opt to start with British Telecom. The phone company combines the efficiency of government bureaucracy with the service ethos of the Mafia, all delivered with the joviality of a Barbary pirate. I call BT's toll-free number on my cellphone and connect with a customer service agent.

"I'm sorry, sir, but there is no record of that house," I am told.

"What do you mean?"

"Your address doesn't exist."

Nice little *Twilight Zone* touch, that. "I'm sitting right here. Of course it exists."

"Perhaps you've made a mistake, sir."

Keeping her on the line, I take my lease and go to speak with my landlord directly. In addition to owning several rental properties in town, Andy also runs the main tourist marina in Henley, which happens to be located adjacent to Boathouse Reach.

As I round the corner, the marina staff is busy topping up the petrol tanks and scrubbing the poop deck of a large sternwheeler tour boat moored at the dock. It is perhaps a hundred feet long and twenty-three feet abeam. The hull is painted blue and the top decks white. Its name, *The New Orleans*, is inscribed in gold and black just below the pilot's cabin. A pair of thick smokestacks and a stern paddlewheel complete the Mississippian allusion.

The marina office is housed in a small brick building set back from the river; Andy is sweeping the front stoop with a broom. As I approach, I hold up the lease. "Is this the correct address?"

Andy glances at the document. "Yes it is."

By now, Miss BT is losing her icy charm. "Could you repeat the postal code?"

"RG9. That's R as in Robert, G as in George…"

"Oh! I thought you said B as in Bob! Here it is…"

Normally I don't give in to psychological torture so fast, but this one's good. I quickly agree to all her offers of additional service, including broadband, voice mail, caller ID, and monthly carpet shampoos. "Thank you for calling BT."

I hang up. Andy takes one look at the tears streaming down my cheeks. "You look like you could use a pint."

We walk around the corner to the Anchor. The interior roof of the pub is approximately five and a half feet tall, although much of this clearance is obstructed by thick oak timbers. Black-and-white photos, including one of a much younger Andy and his oar mates manning a scull, decorate the walls. We take our beers and retreat to a small garden at the rear of the pub that has been planted with wisteria and rose bushes. Andy tilts his glass in my direction. "Welcome to Henley."

I take a sip of my beer. It is nutty and sweet, and very delicious. I turn my attention back to my host. "Have you lived here long?"

"All my life." In fact, as Andy explains, his ancestors first came to the area some five hundred years ago, just after the last plague created numerous openings in the river transport business. In addition to towing corn barges into London, his family has owned pubs, hotels, and docks along the river. His grandfather founded the marina and Andy hopes to pass it down to his son.

I have found in my travels that there are two types of people in life: those who never stray far from home, and those who are always eager to see what's over the next hill. If you don't know which you are, here's an easy quiz. Do you live less than ten ki-lometres from your parents? Did you go to kindergarten with a sizeable number of your adult friends? Are most of your religious holidays spent deciding who is going to cook the turkey and invite Uncle Vince? If you answer yes to two out of three, then you are likely the former.

Personally, I fall into the latter category. I don't live within a thousand kilometres of my family, most of my kindergarten friends were in jail by Grade Three, and I would just as soon spend Christmas Day lying on a beach in Australia roasting my hide as basting a bird. "Have you ever wanted to live anywhere else?" I ask Andy.

He shakes his head. "I'm already living in the best place in the world. Why should I leave?"

That evening, after dinner, I pour myself a large glass of wine and step out onto the front balcony. The sun is just setting below the Chiltern Hills to the west, and the trees across the way are lit in a fiery orange light. Ducks bob on the sparkling surface of the river, occasionally disappearing as they chase a minnow below. Far in the distance, white clouds billow across the horizon.

I sip my wine and ponder Andy's attachment to Henley. I have never understood how someone could limit an entire life to one country, let alone one village. As I ponder the vagaries of the human heart, a full moon rises over the distant hills, its white face reflecting upon the Thames. The swans head for the shore. Even though they could stretch their wings and fly to the farthest corner of the earth, they clamber up onto the marina pavement, tuck their heads beneath one wing, and fall into slumber—at peace and content. I suspect that even a rolling stone could be inspired to stop upon this restful sanctuary, lulled by the beauty and tranquility. Will this paradise capture our hearts too?

2

SEPTEMBER

Meeting the Locals

The British, in case you weren't aware, are an eccentric lot.

Exhibit A is the biker gang that has congregated outside the Angel pub. In Canada, a crowd of bikers consists of a dozen or so hairy guys on Harleys comparing tattoos. In Britain, they are lardy sales reps on mirror-covered Vespas comparing hemorrhoid treatments. I honestly can't decide which I prefer more.

It is a crisp, sunny morning, the first Saturday in September, and I am on my way to *THE BIG ONE*, a boot sale being held across the river on the regatta meadow. From what I understand, this is a particularly British institution in which people pile effluvia into the rears of their cars and drive several hundred kilometres for the privilege of displaying it in an open field. Likewise, customers travel a similar distance in order to view, and presumably buy, said items.

I give the Mods a wide berth and head for the bridge. The two lanes that lead across the narrow span are clogged with cars, buses, and trucks. A large sign bolted to the railing of the bridge states "Warning. Engine drivers must only take one loaded truck at one time over this bridge. Drivers are responsible for damages." I count at least three immense trucks stationary on the span and tiptoe across.

At the boot sale, several hundred cars and vans are parked on the grass in long lines, each one sporting a table or two jammed with all manner of toy soldiers, LPs, used clothing, and antiquated sporting equipment. I pause in front of a display of religious rugs. One depicts Mary resting her hand upon a supine lion. I don't recall this specific incident from the Gospels, but I was never much of a biblical scholar, so I give the artist the benefit of the doubt. I'm pretty sure Mary never met Elvis, though.

In general, shoppers have about as much chance of finding a bargain at a boot sale as spotting Gandhi eating a steak, but that doesn't deter them a whit. The love of the pursuit is written in their faces. They are so rapt, so focused, my only wish is that I had a better command of the art of pickpocketing.

To be honest, the British are not exactly top-of-the-league when it comes to bargaining. The best haggler I have ever met was David, a Lebanese accountant raised in Texas. He once took me to a flea market in Paris where, in a broad nasal twang, he proceeded to bargain with a Russian *brocanteur* by banging an antique hand grenade sitting on the table.

The British, however, are far too taciturn to exhibit such brio. I am standing in front of a wicker chair that has had its seat burst, possibly by an impressive display of flatulence. Plainly, it has no better use than firewood, yet a burly farmer is coyly offering £20 for it. The seller notes that the chair is a genuine Louis XIX, and he wouldn't part with it for less than £30. By now, David would have been taking a hacksaw to the leg of either the chair or the vendor, but the farmer meekly offers £25, which is grudgingly accepted. The look on his face as he clutches his treasure in his massive arms is so tender in its naivety that I decide to sell him Henley Bridge right then and there. But, alas, it is time to return home, as I am awaiting a delivery from the John Lewis department store in Reading.

When I reach my front door, two stout men are unloading our new barbecue; the Thermos Sierra x150 comes complete with dual turbo burners, electronic starter, chromed implement rack, and convertible hood. Fortunately for the Henley fire brigade, it is completely assembled; all that is required is meat.

A brisk, five-minute walk puts me at the door of the butcher shop on Duke Street. I glance through the beaded curtain door; the store contains an impressive array of fresh rack of lamb, pork ribs, chicken breast, and beefsteak, all lovingly displayed beneath the sneeze-proof countertops. Mr. Trowbridge, the owner of the establishment, is dressed in a white apron and traditional pork pie hat. He is a barrel-chested man with a prominent brow and a pair of hands sufficiently large to dispatch an ox, should he happen by chance upon a tasty one. I wait until he finishes with the previous customer before making my request.

"You wouldn't happen to have three kilograms of pork ribs, would you?" I ask.

Trowbridge tilts his hat back. "Special occasion, is it?"

"I'm christening a new barbecue."

"I have just the thing, young man." Mr. Trowbridge rummages about in his walk-in cooler and returns with a smoked side of pork casually tucked under one arm. Placing it on a well-worn wooden block, he grasps a huge knife and proceeds to cleave. The resulting portions are nothing like the skeletal remnants pawned off as ribs in a supermarket; these have more in common with pork chops, each bone a mere footnote to the chunky crown of marbled meat. "Look all right?" he asks.

I indicate my approval by drooling on the counter. I pay at the till and head back home.

There is an art to cooking. My first rule of thumb is not to cut off my thumb, or for that matter anything else I might miss in later years. After that, the rest is just details.

Since Mr. Trowbridge has already been so kind as to reduce the meat to its constituent ribness, I proceed directly to mixing

Gord's Secret Rib Sauce. I must say in all modesty that I make the best rib sauce you will ever taste. I marinate the ribs for one hour in one cup of brown sugar, half a cup of soy sauce, a quarter cup of mustard, two teaspoons of ground black pepper, one teaspoon of hot sauce, and eight cloves of crushed garlic. I brown the ribs over low heat on the barbecue, then place them with the marinade in a pan and roast them uncovered in the oven at 150°c for thirty minutes.

The second-most enjoyable aspect of this meal, right after eating it, is annoying the neighbours. As the marinade and fat drip off the ribs, it sends up an aroma that wafts for hundreds of metres in all directions. As I roast the meat, a steady stream of people wanders by. I can observe their faces as they catch a whiff of this ambrosia, turning their heads this way and that until they identify the source of their torment. I wave my tongs, but they always avert their gaze in embarrassment, aware that they have been observed coveting my dinner in a carnal fashion. It's so easy to tease the British, really.

I am just about finished when a tall, dark-haired man of about thirty walks up to my patio and introduces himself. His name is Alan, and he lives only a few doors down. "What's that you're cooking? It smells very good."

"Ribs. Would you like to try one?"

"I'd be delighted."

I pick up a rib that has been sufficiently browned and hand it across. While this may sound charitable on my part, it really is a rotten thing to do. "How does it taste?"

Alan cleans the meat off down to the bone and is contemplating sucking on the marrow. "Marvellous. Where are you from, by the way?"

"Canada. And yourself?"

"Lived in Henley all my life."

"You must really enjoy it here."

"Awful place, really. You wouldn't have one more rib to spare, would you?"

I ignore the bad pun and hand over another morsel. Alan finishes it almost as expeditiously. I am awaiting his request for thirds when he surprises me with an invitation. "Have you gone for a cruise on the river yet?"

I admit that I haven't.

"You must try it sometime."

"Why?"

Alan ponders for a moment. "Ever read *Three Men in a Boat*?"

"Can't say as I have."

Alan generously hands me back the rib bone. "Get back to me when you do."

"You bet! I'll put it right on top of my 'to do' list." When hell gets a hockey club, that is. My sole experience navigating a watercraft occurred several years ago, while prospecting for gold in Lake of the Woods, Ontario. In order to reach some of the more remote islands, I puttered through miles of interlocking lakes in a sixteen-foot aluminum boat, enjoying the pristine waters and sunshine, until one day a summer storm caught me mid-lake. Cranking the twenty-horsepower outboard to its full throttle, I ran for shore, dodging thunderbolts as they struck the water all around me. Since then, I have developed a phobia of all things nautical.

I wave amicably as Alan recedes.

The following Friday dawns sunny and bright. I make my way up Station Road toward the newsagent through a cool mist that clings to the pavement, imparting a glistening patina. Inside, Vinodhan the newsagent is busy examining Tara, a buxom young woman gamboling topless in the surf on page three of the *Sun*.

Vinodhan is originally from Bangladesh where, oddly enough, few women gambol in such fashion, and it interests him greatly. He pauses long enough from his studies of Western culture to sell me a copy of the local newspaper.

The *Henley Standard* has been published every Friday morning for the last 130-odd years. It is a tabloid of some sixty-four pages, filled with the flotsam and jetsam of local life, an inky peephole into the soul of a community.

I take advantage of the fine fall day to read my copy on a bench adjacent to the river. The front page of most newspapers is reserved for murder and other calamity, but the lead story in this morning's *Standard* is a rather sad tale regarding conkers. It seems that local youth have abandoned the age-old pastime of tying a string through chestnuts and whacking each other on the knuckles. A task force has discovered that the tykes now favour video games and Internet pornography, a revelation if there ever was one.

I move on to a story about a bird that had to be rescued from a tree. It seems a Harris hawk got caught up in a columnar poplar when the falconer's straps on its legs became enmeshed in the branches. It was hanging upside down for several hours before the fire brigade could arrive with an extension ladder—at 2 AM, no less—and free the animal. They are now looking for the rightful owner—to give him the bird, so to speak.

I am distracted by a man wresting with technology. He is in his mid-forties, dressed in a dark wool suit, and is equipped with a professional digital camera the size of a bowling ball. His head bobs up and down, like one of those plastic cartoon statues on the rear window of a car, as he fusses with the dozen or so knobs and buttons on the casing. "Bloody thing."

"Need any help?"

The photographer holds up the camera. "Yeah, do me a favour and toss this useless thing in the river."

I introduce myself as a Canadian journalist sojourning in Henley, and Richard, who is the editor of the *Standard*, explains his mission is to capture some fall colour along the Thames. It is 1 PM, however, so Richard invites me to the Angel for a liquid lunch instead. This is the first time I have been inside the pub. It is very old, with a bleached pine floor that would put a roller coaster to shame, and walls painted blood red for reasons upon which I choose not to speculate. We are the only patrons in the bar, except for two undergraduate students sitting at the bay window exchanging psychology notes and lewd banter.

Richard buys a round of Brakspear Bitter, which, unfortunately, recently closed its brewery in town after 178 years. "They're great brewers and lousy pub owners, so they licensed off the brewing and kept all the pubs." The beer is now made in the North and shipped down, much to nobody's delight.

I take a sip. To my untrained Canadian tongue, it tastes full-bodied with a hint of cream.

Richard takes a sip and sighs. "It's too thin, and bitter. They say they're trying to get it right, but..." He lets the thought trail off, the expression on his face saying it all. There are fewer bonds stronger than the one between an Englishman and his pint, and woe to he who tries to sunder it.

I ask Richard about the man who struts about town in a green military beret and camouflage pants.

"Oh, that's Colonel Bogey—he's mad. He used to parade around with a fake gun but someone who didn't know called the police. Of course, they show up and he wouldn't come out of his house so they put it under siege." Eventually the misunderstanding was cleared up without mayhem, but the police confiscated his gun and the colonel is now reduced to marching about town with a golf umbrella, which must be a bit of a letdown.

I explain that I've decided to write a book about my experiences in Henley, an idea that Richard finds most agreeable. "If you'd like, I'll set up a few meetings with the more colourful people in town," he says.

I express my gratitude and offer to buy another round, but Richard finishes his beer, shakes my hand, and abruptly rises. "Must be off. I'll get back to you in a few days." He heads back down the riverbank, stopping now and again to curse at his camera. With any luck, he may catch an upside-down raptor eating a conker.

My chance encounter with Richard motivates me into doing a bit of research on Henley-on-Thames. The town library is located at the north end of the vast expanse of asphalt that constitutes Waitrose's car park. It is a modern building of brick and blue carpet, with large skylights and oodles of computers. But all the modern gloss can't cover up the smell of mouldy wool emanating from the cranks who make this haven their home.

Upon entering the library, I am immediately impressed not only by the quality of Henley's oddballs, but the quantity. Male garb consists of fetching plaid cardigans covered in calcified brown sauce, while the women tend to sport nylon support hose and Safeway bags. They are variously employed at snoozing and giving baleful glances at the urchins who run riot in the children's section. There is something reassuring about their presence, like lichen on an oak tree.

I ask the nearest woman in brown tweed for help and she directs me to the historical section. The shelf is overflowing with weighty tomes on Oxfordshire, but my eye comes to rest upon a book labelled *The Chilterns*. It is a history of the surrounding hills written by two landscape geographers, Leslie Hepple and Alison Doggett. It is replete with pictures of earnest Victorian archaeologists pointing to clay pits, woodland glens, sixteenth-century county maps, and knobby Iron Age forts. According to Hepple, one of the most ancient remnants of man in the UK was found just northeast of here, near High Wycombe. It is the carbonized remains of a Neanderthal cooking pit that dates back at least one hundred thousand years. In spite of the Neanderthals' brutish appearance, archaeological evidence points to an advanced society with a penchant for ritualistic burial rites, sophisticated pottery, and complex communication skills. In fact, one theory claims that the Neanderthal race did not die out twenty-five thousand years ago at all, but became absorbed into modern *Homo sapiens* stock. I can't help but think that this would go a long way to explaining the appearance of Mr. Trowbridge.

I gather up a pile of books and sit down at a desk near an elderly man who is either having a nap without breathing or dead; either way, he doesn't interrupt my research. Henley, it turns out, wasn't mentioned in the *Domesday Book*, so it either didn't exist in 1086, or was hiding. Regardless, the site was the highest navigable point up the Thames for commercial barges during the Middle Ages, and a settlement officially appeared shortly thereafter. By 1150, the area featured a lively market for grain and lumber destined for the London market, four days away by barge. There was no bridge or church, but the community did have an open sewer ditch by 1170, something that must have made them very relieved.

St. Mary's Church dates from circa 1220. During the thirteenth century, indulgences were granted to parishioners who paid for a church's rebuilding or upkeep. An indulgence remitted a specified number of days from purgatory, the waiting room between Heaven and Hell where last-chancers chilled their heels. The deal was so popular among Henley citizens that sufficient funds were raised to build a chapel within a year.

Henley held its first official town barbecue in 1462, when James Wyllys, a weaver from Bristol, was captured by the Crown and burnt alive for Lollardry. The Lollards were followers of John Wycliffe, a priest from Oxford. Wycliffe stated that there was no scriptural justification for papal authority or indulgences and noted that the transubstantiation was idolatry and nonsense. Well, you don't want that sort of thing catching on, do you? Small wonder why they burned his followers. As Wyllys stood scorching, he hurled a curse upon the town, and 229 promptly succumbed to the plague.

It is my opinion that this is the sort of thing they ought to put in tourist brochures more often. Finishing with my studies, I am merrily noodling through a volume on forms of public execution when the librarian approaches. "I see you have an interest in local culture," she says.

I'm not quite sure where disembowelment fits into the local scene, but I nod amicably. She hands me a slim volume entitled *Three Men in a Boat*, by Jerome K. Jerome. "I recommend you read this."

"What's it about?" I ask.

"Three men in a boat. It's quite amusing."

I get the distinct impression that three men knitting a sweater would amuse her immensely. I thank her profusely and attempt to put it back on the shelf while she's not looking, but I notice that the CCTV camera mounted on the wall is following me. I sigh and check the book out. Maybe it will come in handy whacking spiders.

"I am writing to let you know we have no record of a TV licence at this address."

I'm feeling rather guilty today. According to the notice I've received in the mail, I've been watching TV illegally for almost a month now. From what I can make out, I must pay more than a hundred quid for the honour and privilege of watching the fictionalized lives of working-class residents in East London, documentaries on toads, and adverts for sanitary napkins. "If you are watching TV without a valid licence," the letter continues, "you could be breaking the law, and be liable to a fine of up to £1,000 and a good trouncing with a cricket bat."

Just to be on the safe side, I turn on the radio. The BBC informs me that this is the anniversary of the Battle of Britain. For the most part, I find any information imparted on radio to be one step above the veracity of political statements, but I am intrigued nonetheless, primarily because of the map spread before me on the dining-room table. It is an Ordnance Survey map of the Henley area, a rather splendid document containing a wide assortment of useful information including golf courses and country pubs (each one marked with a little blue pint). What is especially interesting is the secret Spitfire factory, labelled, cryptically enough, "Secret Spitfire Factory." It sits on the Berkshire side of the Thames, less than a mile from my home.

As I pore over the map, I have one ear cocked to the radio documentary. During the summer of 1940, Hitler was preparing to invade England with an amphibious assault codenamed "Sea Lion." Before the Germans could launch an invasion, however, they needed to gain control of the air. By August 1940, bombing raids involving nearly fifteen hundred Luftwaffe aircraft a day swept over southern England, targeting seaports, air bases, and defence facilities.

On paper, it looked like an uneven match. The RAF's Fighter Command had only six hundred interceptors to pit against the oncoming wave, but they had one big advantage—the Spitfire. First built in 1938, the fighter was the ideal interceptor. Sleek, lightweight, and hugely powerful, it could climb to forty thousand feet and cruise at 360 mph. When the Battle of Britain reached its height in September 1940, it was bringing down as many as 185 enemy aircraft a day with its armament of .303-inch machine guns.

Unfortunately, the RAF lost quite a few of their own planes and instigated a secret program to replace them. During the height of the battle, Welsh miners dug a tunnel into the chalky flanks of White Hill near Henley, far away from the prying eyes of Nazi spies. Every day, workers at this tunnel and dozens of other sites throughout the UK churned out Spitfires. In the end, the British won the battle through the simple expediency of shooting down German bombers faster than Germany could finish off Spitfires. By the spring of 1941, after losing some seventeen hundred aircraft, Hitler turned his attention to Russia and postponed his invasion of England—forever, as it turned out.

It is a chilly day, and the clouds roiling up the valley threaten imminent rain, but the drops hold off as I ride my bicycle south along Wargrave Road, in search of this mysterious facility. For the first few hundred yards, the road is mostly flat, meandering through meadows and horse pasture, but the river soon cuts close to the base of White Hill, forcing the road to rise up the steep pitch. I huff and puff my way uphill for a short way until I come to an unmarked junction. Turning left, I follow a narrow road leading deep into the thick forest covering the slope. I reach a clearing at the end of the road.

I spot no sign saying "Secret Spitfire Factory," just a large white van. A portable skid next to the truck is piled high with cardboard storage boxes. They contain records for a large multi-national bank, the kind of things that spies like to peek at, so I assume I am at the right spot. I am closing a box just as a cheerful Irish man with short-cropped ginger hair appears and politely says, "What the *feck* do you think you're doing then?"

I explain that I am writing a book, which is always an excellent excuse with the Irish when you're caught bare-assed messing about in places you shouldn't be. "Is this the old Spitfire factory?"

"Yes, it is." He is quite proud of the fact, but he won't invite me in because he quite rightly assumes I'd have my nose shoved into whatever they're confidentially storing the first moment his back is turned. He is more than happy to let me peer in from the entrance, however, which consists of a set of blast-proof steel doors affixed to the side of the hill by massive hinges. Inside, a square tunnel five metres high and five metres wide stretches for about a kilometre into the hill, the end lost from view by a gentle curve to the left. The ceiling is twenty centimetres of reinforced concrete and the walls are brick. I imagine it was originally designed as one huge conveyor belt, with the guts of the fuselage stuck in way at the back, and the final bits, like the bullets and RAF sticker badge, sitting right here by the front door, ready to be slapped on just before they flew off.

I thank the clerk for his help and pedal into town feeling rather ambivalent about the fate of the secret factory. On the one hand, a genuine artifact of one of the most decisive battles in Britain's history has been turned into a repository for dusty cheque stubs. On the other hand, it could be worse; I hear McDonald's is looking for a new outlet near town, and their conveyor belt would feel quite at home there.

As I head back, the skies finally open up and I find myself pedalling into a fierce wall of rain. One thing I notice about Henley: it's brilliant when it comes to dull weather. Not your simple, plebeian showers here; an entire range of meteorological expression, from sodden downpour to North Sea blizzard, is perpetually on the menu. In between major cloudbursts, of course, is a wide selection of drizzle, mists, spits, and dust-settlers. It's no small wonder that moss grows in thick green clumps on the mortar between the bricks on my garden wall.

I wish I had borrowed Colonel Bogey's umbrella. By the time I reach home, the rain has worked its way through my anorak and is running in a constant rivulet down the cleft of my derriere. I peel off my garments, throw on a bathrobe, and set the kettle on the stove to brew up a hot cup of tea. From the way the rain is lashing against the windowpanes, it is obvious that any further expeditions are out for the day. I don't feel like writing in my diary; instead, I take my brew upstairs and settle into the living-room couch.

Three Men in a Boat is sitting on the coffee table adjacent to the couch, exactly where I abandoned it after returning from the library several weeks ago. I open the book and note that it's now one week overdue.

I flip idly through the pages. The book is a novel, set in the form of a travel journal. Just before the end of the nineteenth century, when steam launches were beginning to dominate river travel, the author decided to take a fifteen-foot skiff on a pleasure cruise with two of his bachelor friends, Harris and George, and his dog, Monty. The idea was to row upstream along the Thames from Kingston to Oxford. Much to my surprise, I find the story enchanting and read through it avidly. Amid various adventures, they gradually work their way up the river until they come to camp one night upstream from Henley, where Harris imbibes Scotch and gets attacked by a flock of bloodthirsty swans.

I look out the front window. A gaggle of the feathery bastards has gathered in front of Andy's marina. Tradition has it that Richard the Lionheart brought them back to England during the Crusades. They were placed under the protection of the Crown and could only be consumed with special permission from the monarch. The birds were considered quite delicious and it was a sign of high station to have them at a banquet, stuffed with a succession of smaller birds, from quail and pheasant to duck and goose, kind of like a poultry babushka doll.

I dub this particular group of juvenile swans "The Craps." Like many teenagers with raging hormones, they have formed a gang so that they can be miserable together. They mark their territory with large mounds of green shit and pull white feathers from their butts, which is, I suspect, the avian equivalent of "*Yo momma!*" They spend the better part of the day terrorizing small dogs that wander too close. It could be worse, I suppose; at least they can't afford spray paint. It's a pity that Queen Elizabeth doesn't have a fondness for swans, because we could use a royal barbecue or two to thin out the ranks.

I return to my book. Before I know it, the afternoon has passed, and I am thoroughly entranced with the notion of touring the Thames. Perhaps I should take up Alan's offer of a boat trip, after all.

I read an article in the *Times* a few years back about a two-thousand-year-old corpse that they found in the bogs. Apparently, the remains were so well-preserved that they were able to extract a DNA sample from the tissue. Researchers then examined specimens from people all over the world in order to trace its descendants. They discovered that the nearest living relatives were half a kilometre from where they found the corpse. I can just imagine what they said upon hearing the news. "Oh, that must have been Uncle Nigel. He disappeared one night coming home from the pub."

Small towns in England used to be like that. Andy's ancestors arrived hereabouts during the Great Plague, and I suspect Edwina's forebears were probably eviscerating sacrificial virgins up in the Chilterns during the Bronze Age. But a significant cultural invasion is also taking place since the Second World War. Mo, the man who runs the kebab place, is from Turkey, and Vinodhan the newsagent hails from Bangladesh. My neighbour, Professor Dihatsu, is from Japan, and Alan's wife, Niina, comes from Finland.

So it comes as no great surprise when I meet Mavis from Africa.

I am sitting in Osvaldo's hairdressing salon covered in a black sateen cape. Osvaldo is a tiny Lithuanian man dressed in a black T-shirt and cat's-eye glasses. He purses his lips and places one finger on his chin and contemplates my hair in consternation.

Osvaldo has reason for concern. When I woke up this morning, my head looked like something that would not be out of place in a zombie movie. Large gobs of gel were useless; I finally had to resign myself to scaring children and small dogs for the rest of my life or getting a haircut.

Osvaldo pokes and prods at my hair, much like a raven picking at a chunk of road pizza. He sighs at length then finally announces that there is only one person who might be able to manage my unruly follicles. He claps his hands twice, and his chief hairdresser emerges from the back room.

Mavis, a large-boned black woman with a pretty smile, gently pushes Osvaldo to one side like a rag doll. She grips my head firmly in her large hands and twists it one way, then the other.

"What you do to your hair? It look like you comb it with a rake!" She laughs a big, hearty laugh then picks up a long, thin pair of scissors and begins to snip away extraneous bits in professional fashion. "Don't you worry, honey, Mavis will have it looking good in no time."

Mavis's accent reminds me of the Caribbean, but it is not as lilting. I listen as she tells me about a recent visit back home to see her family. "It was marvellous! I saw my children and all their aunties and uncles."

"How was the weather?"

"Fantastic!" She pats her cheeks. "Can't you tell? I got some colour!"

"Where is home, anyway?"

Mavis points to a pin on her lapel. It sports a small flag, one I don't recognize. "I am from Zimbabwe."

I am surprised that she would forsake the comforts of Henley for the dangers of Harare, and say so.

Mavis waves her scissors dismissively in the air. "It's not as bad as people think. It's a beautiful place, if people only knew."

Everything I had been hearing lately—election riots, Robert Mugabe's marauding thugs—indicated otherwise. "Were there any food shortages when you were there?"

"Oh yes, but we all share."

"How about petrol?"

Mavis laughs. "My poor husband! He spends half the day pushing his car around to the pumps!" Mavis finishes and brushes me down. I admire my hair; just as Osvaldo promised, she has done a lovely job. I tip her well and head out the door, idly wondering why the nicest people always end up with the worst leaders. At least Mavis has Henley as a refuge.

When I get back home, there is a message on my answering machine from Alan; he says it is a perfect day for a boat outing. I swallow my reservations regarding small watercraft and call back, and we agree to go out later that morning. The son of a plumber, Alan has the wonderful ability to see the world through a child's eyes then convert those imaginative impressions into highly profitable businesses. Although only in his mid-thirties, he is semi-retired, having sold his digital TV firm for several million pounds a few years ago.

Alan has never owned a boat because, in his own words, they are a damned nuisance. "Do you know what the best two days of owning a boat are?" he asks. "The first and the last."

Instead, he has acquired a boat for the day from Andy's marina. It is a rather squat, four-and-a-half-metre fibreglass launch equipped with a nifty wooden steering wheel that makes me want to squint like a pirate and say "*AAR!*" when I spin it. The launch is powered by an inboard diesel that emits a low rumble and an oily stench when the dock jockey turns it over. An oar, sawn in half, has been kindly provided for our convenience.

The air is calm and the sky is studded with thick white clouds as we head upstream. Several pedestrians dawdle along on the towpath, but most of the boats moored along the way have already been wrapped under winter tarps. We have the river almost completely to ourselves, which is a good thing as Alan is steering mostly with his feet.

"Driving on the river is a completely different experience," he notes. "If I were going this slow in my car, I'd be arrested." I consider this a sage observation.

We approach Marsh Lock, located about a mile upstream from Henley. We arrive at the lock just as the lower gates swing open. We join three other boats in the thirty-metre-long chamber and moor to one side. The lockkeeper closes the lower gates and opens the upper sluice, and the boats begin to rise.

"Whenever I'm in a lock, I'm always amazed at how dangerous and powerful the river can be," says Alan. He points to the Dutch barge adjacent to us. "That boat weighs ten tons and it's lifted eight feet in less than a minute." While true, I can't help but imagine how much more dangerous it would be if the boat *didn't* rise.

The lockkeeper opens the upper gate, and we continue our journey. A six-metre cabin cruiser passes going the other way. The woman pilot gives us a cheery wave, and we return the favour. Alan points at the departing boat. "Have you ever wondered how bizarre that is?"

"What?"

"Strangers will wave to you when you pass on the river."

I ponder his point. "Perhaps there's something about the freedom of the river that makes them carefree and happy."

Alan shakes his head. "I'm carefree and happy when I walk down the street, but I don't *wave* to people I don't know as they pass by. They'd think I was barking mad."

"What an odd concept."

As we approach Shiplake, Alan steers into a side channel running along the west bank. It is lined with half a dozen estates, most of them twenty- and thirty-room mansions set back on wide manicured lawns. "Growing up in Henley, it was like a tease being surrounded by all this wealth," he says.

"Do you find it a burden?"

"No, an inspiration."

I find this interesting. In the back of my mind, I've always thought that the British looked askance at wealth, perhaps because of the great gulf between middle-class families, like Alan's, and the gentry that own great tracts of land. Perhaps this much-ballyhooed antagonism between Toffs and the Hoi Polloi is a bit overplayed for the sake of the audience.

We rejoin the main channel and steer pass several low islands. They are little more than mud banks on which alder and willows have colonized, providing refuge for the Canada geese that paddle among the exposed roots. According to Jerome's description in *Three Men in a Boat*, he and his comrades camped for the night on the fourth island south of Henley, but I have no way of knowing which that might be. We come to a likely spot near a large willow, however, and moor the boat, tying it up fore and aft to some saplings.

We cut the engine and are immediately surrounded by a deep and comprehensive silence. I suspect that in much of the Thames Valley, you can normally hear the distant *clickety-clack* of a train, or the hum of a car, or the drone of an aircraft far above, but here there is nothing but the lapping of the river against the gunwales and the whisper of the wind in the willows. We munch on tuna and mayo sandwiches and luxuriate in the quietness. We round out our meal with blackberries growing alongside the towpath. While we are picking the fruit, a woman approaches on foot. She is perhaps sixty, with rosy cheeks and sparkling blue eyes. I stop her as she passes. "Excuse me, is this the island where the three men in a boat camped?"

"Oh, no. It was swept away long ago in a flood."

Her comment reminds me that even a river as calm and docile as the Thames contains something wild and untamable. We cast off and point our boat back downriver, toward home. As we sail downstream, the steady, low thrum of the diesel and the hot September sun put us into a state of relaxed lethargy.

I could get used to this.

3

OCTOBER

A Pint at the Leander Club

"There's someone I think you should meet—his name is Teddy."
It is Richard calling. He has taken an active interest in
my writing project, which is a bonus, as it saves me a great deal of
time and effort actually digging up sources, something that every
journalist treasures. "I'd love to," I reply.

"Good. Meet me at the Leander Club at noon. Just make sure
you wear a suit and tie—it's kind of posh."

Since 1829, when a group of young gentlemen first took to
boats in the Thames, Henley has been the centre of competitive
rowing in the UK and, arguably, the planet. As Wimbledon is to
tennis and St. Andrews is to golf, so Henley's Leander Club is
to rowing. Founded more than a century ago, at least one heir
apparent to the throne has since pronounced its Pimm's passable.
If there is anywhere in town where one is to encounter a full con-
tingent of Hooray Harries under sail, or at least oar, this is it.

When I arrive at the Leander Club, a row of Ferraris, Porsches,
and Aston Martins are parked in front. I detour around a bright
yellow Lamborghini and enter. Inside, the marble-lined foyer is
decorated with a large board detailing the various Olympic and
world champions who have emanated from the hallowed hall
through the last century.

Richard is in the bar upstairs quaffing a pint with an elderly
man. Teddy's back is bent and his pale blond hair is almost white,
but his blue eyes are still sharp. He wears a Leander blue blazer

decorated with brass buttons, initialed *LC*. In a voice just short of a bellow, he asks, "Would you cah to sit down heah?" The letter R rarely appears in his vocabulary, nor does the letter I. "Would you cah for a glass of what wane?" he asks.

"No, just a Brakspear."

"Bahtendah!" he shouts. "Fetch my good man a beah."

I take an instant liking to Teddy. While waiting for our drinks, he quickly fills me in on his background. Born in 1921 to a Derbyshire vicar, his family moved to Henley when he was three after his father inherited the princely sum of £250,000 from a spinster aunt. By his own admission, Teddy was an indifferent scholar and an avid rower—regardless, his academic and sports pursuits were cut short by the Second World War. He joined the RAF and became a bomber pilot, flying Dakotas in Egypt and seeing action in El Alamein.

We are joined by Peter, Teddy's neighbour and oldest friend. He is a large man, wearing a vest that is intricately patterned with splotches of tomato soup. He bends toward me in conspiratorial fashion. "Did Teddy tell you he was almost court-martialled during the war?"

My attention immediately picks up. "No."

"Teddy was flying light bombers in the Aegean and was told to go out and do some reconnaissance and report back. There he was, flying over the sea, when he spots a German radio tower on an island. Well, he opens up with his cannon and shoots it to bits. He returns to base, thinking they're going to give him the Victoria Cross or something, but his group captain is furious. He said, 'That was the *one* Jerry radio station that was so badly calibrated that it's always sending out the wrong information, and now you've pranged it!'"

Teddy shakes his head sadly, "It seems I wasn't paying attention at briefing."

Peter arches his immense eyebrows at his friend. "The war would have been over much sooner if you'd have just joined the Germans, Teddy."

Peter and Teddy insist upon several more rounds of ale and a few brandy snifters, and it is mid-afternoon by the time I depart from the club, eager for a little fresh air. The first few days of October have been cold, but the wind has shifted to the south and a warm breeze carries the smell of wet leaves and forest moss. The sun, lower now on the horizon, is still strong enough to warm the skin as it shines pale and yellow in a faint blue sky, and I am filled with a desire to experience as much of the remaining day as possible. It is thus with little surprise that I find my feet, on their own accord, turning in the direction away from town.

I follow the towpath that runs downstream toward Hambleden Lock. It is a rather civilized trail, level and straight and paved with rough asphalt. I am accompanied some distance by a lone sculler until he enters the centre of the channel and the current carries him swiftly downstream. With his departure, I find that I have the river all to myself. The miles tumble by in lone contentment until I reach Temple Island, about halfway to Hambleden Lock. It is little more than an islet in the middle of the channel, and it would be quite unexceptional except for the Greek temple that sits on the upstream side, its slim, creamy columns supporting a dome that gleams softly in the sun.

I stop to enjoy the peace. The world is so filled with cars honking, jets roaring, people shouting, and radios blaring that one can easily forget how beautiful silence can be. I am miles from the nearest main road, the flight path for Heathrow has been shifted to the east, and even the ducks have shut up for a moment. The sky is milky blue, and the breeze so gentle that it barely riffles the long grass in the meadow across the river. A black cormorant sits at the pinnacle of an ancient, twisted willow tree, surveying the flowing stream with religious calm. Three swans, flying low in formation, race up the river, skimming its surface. It is so quiet that I can hear their laboured breathing as they cleave the air.

And then some two dozen men, clad in green camouflage jackets, emerge from the forest on the far shore and enter an expanse of meadow. They are carrying long-barrelled shotguns hinged at the breach. Black Labs and springer spaniels bound along. The hunters set up a line in the long grass and wait. Several grouse burst into the air, their cover disturbed by approaching beaters. They fly low, dodging, but the guns flash and a bird drops to the ground.

"Bloody arseholes!" Unnoticed, a rambler has come up behind me. He is clad in a heavy wool coat and a checked cloth cap, his creased, jowly face red from the brisk air. He shakes his walking cane in the general direction of the hunters. "They should give the birds guns and let *them* have a go!" I have this sudden mental image of an armed gang of ducks mugging some little old lady for her bread crumbs, but my companion's tirade banishes such whimsy. "Shooting harmless birds! You call that sporting? Just a bunch of weekend scroungers, that's what they are!"

George and his dog, Emma, from nearby Maidenhead, are out for their daily walk. Emma, a bratwurst sausage with four legs and a tail, rears up and plants two muddy paws on my thigh. When the guns crack, she rushes to the shore, ready to dive in and fetch.

"Birds never harm anyone!" George shakes his walking stick in their general direction. "How'd you like it if I shot and cooked you lot?" I make an attempt at conversation, but George continues on with his prattle, oblivious. Since there doesn't seem to be any way of shutting him up, I bid adieu to Emma and march off in the direction of Henley. She stares after me, a forlorn look on her face, and I feel very guilty leaving her alone to listen to George. I wonder if they make earplugs for dogs.

The tranquility of the Thames is the last thing on my mind as, several days later, I sit in a tailback along the A4. I am heading into Reading, waiting to enter a roundabout. This is a handy little device in which traffic can move unimpeded in all directions by simply yielding to anyone approaching on the right. This works well in theory unless it has been poorly designed or everyone else on the road is a pig-headed moron. Several roundabouts exist along the stretch of the A4 between Henley and Reading, and, for some reason that entirely eludes me, both negative attributes come together with predictable effect at the roundabout leading to Sonning. There, the two lanes on the A4 drop to one lane heading west. That means that the left lane is for those ninety-nine cars heading for Reading, and the right lane for that one turning right toward Sonning. Of course, this handy roadwork dodge only works when traffic is light; as soon as rush hour arrives, the lane leading into Reading begins to back up. This doesn't stop the clever lads, however. With breathtaking nonchalance, they hop into the largely vacant right turning lane, sail their silver Mercedes past waiting motorists in the left, and then aggressively muscle their way into the ongoing lane once in the roundabout, causing further delays with their egotistical arrogance.

It is a particularly busy evening, and after about ten minutes of creeping, I have finally entered the roundabout when a black Audi coupe driven by a banker from the City comes roaring up beside me. I am about to boil over in rage when the driver of a white van in front of me, who has been waiting just as long as I, refuses to let this weasel cut in ahead. I quickly sidle up behind, forcing the Audi driver to either sideswipe the pair of us or miss his turn. Dropping his cellphone in fury, he waves his hand in some naughty sign language and goes for a ride around the traffic circle. As we clear the roundabout, I open my window and give the white van the thumbs-up; I can see him grinning in his big square rearview. Who says driving isn't fun any more?

Owen, as usual, is standing in my driveway when I arrive home. Owen works for a company that builds computers in a shop located above the marina's chandlery. He is an affable, overweight Welshman with a hopeless addiction to cigarettes, hence his frequent appearance outside on my doorstep.

"Guess what?" he announces when I pull in. "I bought a boat!"

Owen conducts me inside Andy's boat repair shop next door to examine what is, without a doubt, the most decrepit fourteen-foot fibreglass runabout I have ever seen in my life. The hull is pitted and cracked, the support ribs appear to have been chewed by a beaver, and the bilge is giving off a smell that normally impels the local constabulary to search for a corpse.

I turn to Owen. "You're not actually going out on the water in *this*, are you?"

Owen slaps the outboard motor, which looks like an excellent locale for a gasoline explosion. "I'm going to take it down to the coast and go right to France!"

Owen has asked Kim, Andy's marina engineer, to give it the once over. As soon as Kim enters the garage and takes one look at the boat, the gleam that pirates acquire when they spot a Spanish galleon wallowing low in the water immediately lights up his eyes. "I think we got a bit of work here, Owen," Kim says.

Owen's forehead wrinkles in worry. "Really?"

Kim nods. "I think we should rebuild the floorboards for starters, mate."

"A set of emergency flares and an inflatable life raft would also be good," I offer.

"First things first," says Owen. "I want a set of new decals on the side. You got anything with big shark's teeth?"

Kim grins. "You just put this boat in the water, mate, and I guarantee you'll see more shark's teeth than you'll ever want."

One aspect of rural England that we have yet to savour is the night scene, so I am pleased when Alan telephones several nights later and invites Linda and me along to see Lou Larue, his favourite jazz musician, playing at the Crooked Billet, his favourite country pub. We climb into Niina's Peugeot and head off north. Alan, who is driving, proceeds to take several corners at about three times the posted rate, and in no time at all I am gripping the dashboard with sufficient force to poke several fingers through the vinyl cover.

We soon enter a dense forest whose canopy has grown right over the road, and the effect is not unlike being on a roller coaster. We wend our way for several miles through twisting lanes until we come to the village of Stoke Row, where Alan turns down an even tinier side lane that leads to our destination.

When we finally stop, we are well and truly in the boonies, with only the full moon hanging above for company. The Crooked Billet is a rambling series of brick and plaster buildings covered in ivy. A billet is an old English term for a tent peg, millions of which were manufactured in the village over the course of the centuries. A crooked billet, of course, is one that is bent. This seems an appropriate moniker, because the interior of the pub doglegs from room to room, each one stacked with bottles, logs for the fire, and the occasional table and chair. The main dining room, the one in which Lou will perform, is about twelve metres long and six metres wide. It feels much bigger, however, because the ceiling is one long barrel vault, perhaps four and a half metres high. The walls have been painted claret red, and the wainscoting consists of green plaid cloth. I crack my shin on a large tub filled with old wine corks and get the feeling this is a party place.

We are shown to a table across from the immense fireplace. The menu has a wide selection of meat, fish, and poultry; I order the duck breast glazed in Hoisin sauce and Linda goes for the chicken stuffed with feta and chorizo. Our appetizer, crab and avocado salad, is superb, and the duck melts in my mouth. There's nothing like driving to the middle of nowhere to get a good meal.

While we are eating, the band arrives from London. Lou walks in carrying an electric keyboard that is almost as long as him. He plops it down on a small side table in front of the fireplace and then goes out to fetch some more equipment. In short order, the tiny open space is filled with drums, a bass cello, and several amps. Dave, the tenor sax player, unpacks his instrument and we make room at the end of our table for his reeds. This promises to be an intimate evening.

The waitresses rush around to deliver dessert and fill everyone's glass, then the band gets down to business. Lou sets the melody for a slow jazz tune, and Dave launches into a mellow solo. Rick gets in his licks on cello then passes the lead back to Lou. It is obviously a very talented quartet, even by London standards. I wonder what has brought them out to this backwater.

The band switches from mellow to manic. The drummer launches into a high-tempo number and Dave scorches the room with a tremendous sax solo. Even though there isn't a square inch to dance, the place is rocking, with everyone boogying in their seats. I begin to understand why the pub was so isolated; a Concorde jet could take off right outside and nobody would hear it. The band rolls through a few more songs and then ends the set with a rousing version of "Basin Street Blues" that has everyone clapping and cheering by the time they finish their first set.

While the band has a smoke, Alan and I take the opportunity to step outside for a stretch. "How do they get these guys to come way out here?" I ask.

"It's the owner of the pub," explains Alan. "He knows everybody in the music business. Tons of celebrities come out here all the time."

I glance around but I don't spot anybody even vaguely famous. In fact, the couple sitting at the table adjacent to the band look as though they might have accidentally wandered in from a trailer park. They are in their sixties and wearing matching grey fleecy jackets and the slip-on suede shoes you order from a catalogue. You know how some people come to resemble their dogs after a while? Well, this pair had managed the unenviable trick of resembling each other. They both have lanky blondish hair, round, distended eyes, and long flat faces punctuated by immense teeth. I get the distinct impression there's some hillbilly mojo going on up here in the Chilterns that the Tennessee Society to Prevent Kissing Cousins might want to know about.

Lou and his band return and, without further ado, launch into "House of the Rising Sun." The audience looks like it's about to kick over the furniture and howl at the moon—even the linotype portraits on the wall are jiving. The set flows by in a blur, and in the end, the band gets a rousing standing ovation amid hoots and hollers.

We are settling the bill when Lou comes over. "That was brilliant," I exclaim. "Could you autograph a CD for us?" Lou is more than happy to oblige. At this point, I have several bottles of wine under my belt, and it is, of course, every man's God-given right under the circumstances to make a complete ass of himself. "You know, Lou, you sure attract a weird audience."

The musician looks puzzled. "What do you mean?"

"Didn't you see the bug-eye twins sitting beside you all night?"

"Those are my parents."

I should mention that I have been on a diet for several months, and up to this point had managed to lose half a pound. Within the next five seconds, however, I shrink well past midget size into the realm of garden gnome. In fact, Alan could tuck me into the glove box on the way home, which is well-lit by the glow of embarrassment emanating from my face.

I'm very sensitive, you know; thank goodness I don't write any of this in my diary.

"William Lenthall, speaker of the Long Parliament, was born in this house in 1591."

I have recovered sufficiently from my embarrassment to once again be seen in public and have taken the opportunity to read the various historical signs posted about town.

I am standing outside a rather nondescript home on Hart Street, across from the entrance to St. Mary's Church. I am completely at a loss as to Lenthall's significance and am trying to suss it out when I spot Teddy approaching. He is trundling across the bridge on a four-wheeled electric cart. A tiny Union Jack attached to the carrying basket flaps jauntily; I like to think of it as his Henley-Davidson. He motors over when I wave. "How are you this morning?" he asks.

"Fine, Teddy. I had a wonderful time with you at the club the other day."

"Delightful!" He glances around then lowers his voice to just below bellow level to make sure no one else can overhear. "If you're interested, old boy, I can get you a membership there. You know, pull the right strings and all that."

"That's very nice of you, Teddy, but I don't row." In fact, I find the whole thought of splashing about on the river in Spandex underwear distinctly embarrassing.

"Not to worry; if truth be told, half the membership never lifted an oar in their life. You'd fit right in."

Changing the subject, I point at the sign. "Do you know who this guy is?"

Teddy squints at the sign for a moment. "Of course! Lenthall helped precipitate the Civil War between King Charles and Parliament in 1642." Teddy points up the road with his left hand. "Charles's forces were centred in Oxford to the north." He turns and points his right hand across the bridge. "Cromwell's Roundheads were in London, to the south." Teddy brings his hands together with a resounding smack. "And Henley was right in the middle."

"Did they fight for control of Henley?"

"Indeed they did. Terrible business."

"There was a battle in Henley? I'd love to learn more."

"You should go to the museum. Come along, I'll show you where it is."

Teddy pulls a U-turn and we head along the road that runs beside the Thames. We pass an ancient building that rambles along for half a block. It is a timber and brick construction, the exposed oak timbers bent from centuries of supporting the red clay roof, whose peak now meanders in sinuous fashion.

"It's the old town granary," explains Teddy. "The watermen would row their barges up from London and load up with corn and barley."

We motor on until we come to the River & Rowing Museum, a series of low buildings sitting on cement stilts. I had passed them many times, but taken them for old boat sheds, their wood-clad exteriors bleached to a deep grey by years of exposure to the elements. In fact, the complex is only four years old, built largely from local donations to honour the Thames, the town, and the popular local sport.

I bid adieu to Teddy and go inside. Just off the main entrance is a display dedicated to Britain's Olympic rowing triumphs. A large, airy room is dominated by the two boats that were specially designed for the 2000 Olympic Games in Sydney. A pair of seven-foot bronze statues of Steve Redgrave and Matthew Pinsent rest beside the boats. Redgrave strides along like a Greek hero, an oar clasped over his shoulder like a Hoplite's spear; the only thing missing is a shield and loincloth.

A long, sunlit, elevated walkway takes me to the rear of the museum, where a hall has been dedicated to the history of Henley-on-Thames. As I enter the large room, I am momentarily distracted by an enchanting sight; it is the skeleton of a woman's hand, small and delicate, clutching two silver pennies. The accompanying plaque explains that, after the demise of the Romans, Britain was divided up into various Saxon kingdoms. Henley was at the boundary of three fiefs: Danelaw (Buckinghamshire), Mercia (Oxfordshire), and Wessex (Berkshire). When archaeologists excavated a Roman villa near the present village of Bix, they found the skeleton of a woman who had been hastily buried at the base of an ancient wall. In her hand were the two silver pennies from the reign of Burgred of Mercia (A.D. 874). No evidence explaining the mystery was ever uncovered. Perhaps they never asked Miss Marple.

I continue on to the Civil War display, which features various yellowed diaries, rusty weapons, and posters explaining the conflict. By the time Charles I ascended the throne in 1625, relations between the Crown and Parliament had taken a serious turn. By 1642, the civil war between Charles's royalist army and Cromwell's parliamentarian Roundheads had engulfed Britain. In 1643, Henley indeed became the site of a skirmish. On the night of January 26, royalist forces tried to sneak into the town and capture the bridge over the Thames but were repulsed with a salvo of cannon and blunderbusses. Several royalists were killed or wounded, and the fight subsequently was elevated to the rather grandly titled Battle of Duke Street. The trunk of an oak tree, which bears the remnants of a cannonball from the fracas, is on display as a reminder of the general carnage of war. No word on whether the tree was a royalist, Roundhead, or merely a victim.

Lenthall, of course, was nowhere to be found anywhere near this scrap, and in fact spent the next twenty years agilely trading allegiances until he thankfully died at the ripe old age of seventy-one in Burford, Oxfordshire.

Thanksgiving in Canada traditionally is held in October, unlike the United States, where it is held in November. The festivity is in honour of the colonists who fled to the New World, risking hardship and starvation in order to escape the impiety and intolerance of the Old World. So, it would make sense to celebrate it in Britain, now wouldn't it? Noting a severe lack of horns of plenty or turkey motifs on display at Marks & Spencer, I take it upon myself to establish a new British tradition.

As the day approaches, we invite an English couple over for Thanksgiving dinner. Matthew was born in Canada but came to the UK with his family when he was five; Celia has never been closer to North America than Cornwall. We thought them ideal candidates to introduce to the big bird feast. And so, it is off to Mr. Trowbridge's.

As I exit the door to our home, I spot Owen. His usual sunny disposition has been replaced by a look of gloom. Just to cheer him up, I ask how his boat is proceeding.

"Not good." He leads me around to the marine garage, where his boat, or what is left of it, sits. The hull has been reduced to large, ragged shards of fibreglass and the motor looks as though it has been pounded with a sledgehammer.

"Oh my God," I exclaim. "Did you get hit by a garbage scow?"

Owen shakes his head. "Never even made it to the water."

"What happened?"

"I changed the wheels on the trailer and forgot to tighten the lug nuts." Owen stares at the remains of his boat. "We was doing about 160 down the A3 when they fell off."

"Owen, you're a complete idiot." My commiserations finished, I continue on my journey to the butcher's.

According to a poster in the shop, Mr. Trowbridge offers birds that are raised on free-range farms, spending the day wandering about with little Turkish berets while eating organic worms. Returning home to roost each night, they are bedded down in centrally heated coops and serenaded to sleep with the sound of whispering forests on the stereo. They even get a complimentary haircut before they leave. I have just finished reading all this when I notice a Louisville Slugger hanging on the back wall of Mr. Trowbridge's shop. "You a fan of baseball?" I ask.

"No, that's to protect the till."

I glance over at the impressive array of extremely sharp, large knives behind the chopping block. "Who'd be crazy enough to rob a butcher's shop?"

"It takes all kinds, young man. I was working in a shop a few years back when a thief tried to rob it. One of the lads behind the counter picked up a cleaver and flung it at him. It stuck in the wall about three inches from his nose. If he hadn't missed, it would have split his skull in two." On the upside, it would have made it a lot easier to pick the culprit out of a lineup. I thank Mr. Trowbridge and head home.

The secret to cooking a turkey is to keep it moist and cook it slowly. I always mix a healthy portion of butter and two cans of mandarin oranges into the dressing before stuffing the cavity. By the time Celia and Matthew arrive, the house is filled with the heavenly smell of sage, butter, and bird cooking slowly in the oven. They have brought with them their sons William, age one, and Jack, three. Neither has ever seen snow before so, as a treat, I have prepared two snowballs from the frost in the freezer. Matthew is instantly smitten with his and hurls it off the balcony at the geese with a mighty toss. William, on the other hand, is content to suck on it like an ice cream cone.

When dinner is ready, I am more than happy to show Jack how to make a volcano out of his mashed potatoes and flood the hapless natives below with a flow of hot gravy. William improvises a new hairdo by rubbing his mash in his hair.

We are so engrossed in our meal that we barely notice that the weather has changed. Clouds begin to scud past in a southerly direction, alternatively obscuring the sky with a blanket of dense grey and then opening up a patch of sunlight to illuminate the chestnut trees across the river with a brilliant gold light. It isn't until the wind abruptly increases in velocity that I begin to get alarmed.

It starts with a low moan, shaking the house and making the timbers creak, then a rumble that runs through the attic and pops the attic lid off and sends it crashing to the floor of the upstairs hallway. Rain starts blowing sideways in huge sheets, and the patio furniture is tossed over the railing. The wind has whipped the river into foam.

With a sudden crack, a huge willow tree splits in two and collapses upon a boat moored on the far side of the river. The power goes out, the phones cease, and the satellite dish on our roof is torn off its steel mount and flies away.

All in all, everyone agrees that Canadian Thanksgiving is a jolly idea, even if it is a tad messy.

It is October 31, and Halloween is nigh. The festival dates from around five hundred years before Christ, when the Celts of Ireland marked the New Year at the end of October. They believed it was a time when malignant spirits would try to inhabit the bodies of the living, and so they dressed up in grotesque costumes in an attempt to ward them off. The custom of trick-or-treating dates from the Middle Ages, when children would go from door to door begging for "soul cakes" or currant bread in return for saying prayers for deceased relatives. As far as I'm concerned, any holiday that offers children the opportunity to dress up in disguises and extort candy from adults is okay with me.

Unfortunately, other adults disagree. I am in Waitrose searching for some sweets to pass out later that night when a headline in the *Daily Mail* catches my attention. Apparently, church schools around the country are banning Halloween celebrations amid fears that they could encourage pupils to dabble in Satanism.

"Halloween has obvious connotations with ghosts and ghouls and for that reason it won't be mentioned," says the head of St. Columba's Catholic Primary School in Merseyside.

"Halloween is associated with evil," agrees the headmaster at Banks St. Stephen's Church of England. "We are a church school and the festival throws up problems in its pagan origins."

I turn to find Edwina reading over my shoulder. "About time, too," she says. "There's no telling what mischief children will get up to I always say if you give a child enough rope they'll hang someone with it although *my* nephew was a perfect saint never caused a spot of trouble because if he had then he would have had his little bottom scrubbed let me tell you…"

I glance around casually for a cork, but instead spot a boy with a large metal bolt running completely through his neck. His mother doesn't seem to notice. Her other child, a girl about four, is sporting an immensely distorted set of teeth, with great charm. I can't possibly imagine these two little angels causing anyone any mischief and explain as much.

Edwina arches her eyebrows. "Just wait until they're older. They'll make a *mess* of the town." She gives the children a frosty glare and marches off toward the prunes section. As soon as Edwina disappears from view, I purchase some chocolate bars, checking to make sure she hasn't planted any razor blades in them, then head back home.

As I walk back, I think about the cherished tradition that surrounds Halloween vandalism. As a child, my uncle Oscar would proudly recall tipping over the outhouse behind the one-room schoolhouse in his rural Saskatchewan village (extra points were awarded if the teacher was using it at the time). Sadly, outhouses were long gone by the time I was growing up, and we had to limit ourselves to more mundane activities. Flinging toilet paper rolls over the principal's tree or feeding chocolate-flavoured laxatives to the ill-tempered pit bull on the corner were always popular, but my favourite practical joke involved the lowly potato.

Our neighbour, a bald-headed widower whom we nicknamed Uncle Fester, was always threatening to shoot any child who ventured onto his property in search of cherries or apples from his trees. One late October night, under cover of darkness, we inserted a spud into the tailpipe of his Ford Edsel then hid in the bushes. Fester soon emerged and started his car. As was his wont, he revved the engine to warm it up, building up back pressure in the exhaust system until the potato exploded from the rear end with a tremendous bang. We crouched in glee, eagerly expecting him to burst a cranial valve, but, much to our chagrin, he nonchalantly put the car into gear and drove off, dribbling tater tots. Some people just have no sense of humour.

Owen is standing outside my house having a fag as I come up the front walk. By now, he has forgotten all about his boat mishap and has returned to his usual, cheerful outlook. "What are you all smiley about?" he asks.

"I was just thinking of Halloween. Did you ever get up to any pranks as a kid?"

"Did we! Me an' my mates used to go air-baggin'."

I'm not quite sure I hear him right. "Did you say 'hare-bagging?'"

"No, *air*-baggin'. We'd sneak into the parking lot of the Vauxhall works and whack the side of the new cars with an orange

61

road cone. *Pouff!* It would set off the side air bags. Them security guards would chase us all over the lot. Man, I thought one old codger was going to have a heart attack!" Obviously, the thought of massive financial damage with the potential for death thrown in also warms his heart, and a big grin breaks out over Owen's face. It's a magical holiday.

The wind has dropped and the sun has poked out from behind the clouds, so I drop off the candies and set off on a walk. I round the corner and pass through the marina, where I am confronted by the sight of Kim's feet sticking out from beneath a golf cart. I stop and ask if he's taken up the game.

"Wot, me? Wouldn't be caught dead playin' golf," he says.

"So what's with the cart?"

"Some kids stole it from the course up the hill and tried to leap the river. I pulled it out of the water and claimed salvage." I leave the mechanic, pleased to hear about such initiative and daring on the part of the young.

I cross the bridge and head south along Wargrave Road. Andy's winter dry dock is bustling with activity. Around five dozen boats have been towed into a line adjacent to a twenty-tonne crane. I stand well back to observe. Sliding a double sling made of strong nylon beneath the hull, Andy and his men lift a forty-foot inboard cruiser from the water. Using ropes, the men guide it through the air until it is positioned over stacks of hardwood beams. It is then slowly lowered down until the hull rests securely in the cradle. The entire process takes less than ten minutes.

As I stand watching, Derek, Andy's marina manager, rides up on a bicycle. He is awkwardly clutching a bright blue, vinyl-covered cushion under one arm. "A couple of drunks clambered onto *The New Orleans* last night and threw all the deck furniture into the Thames," he explains. "We'll be plucking cushions out of the water for weeks."

I promise to keep an eye out for wayward furniture and head back into town, admiring how the high-spirited youth of Henley must serve as a shining example for the rest of the country. By the time I get home, darkness has fallen. I pour the candy into a bowl and wait for the first trick-or-treaters to come by.

Their arrival is heralded not by the usual doorbell but by a sharp knock on the riverside of the house. Curious, I go out onto the balcony. *Crack.* An egg explodes just above my head and I am covered with goo. A group of young lads are standing near the road guffawing loudly. "Hey, you twerps!" Another rotten egg hits the wall above my hand. I scramble for cover as they run laughing into the night.

I curse the slack-mouthed yobs and their mothers as I wipe the stinking, slimy goo off my hair. I turn off the porch light and all the rest of the lights in the house, then sit in the darkness and eat my Kit-Kats. Rotten little bastards. What's wrong with kids today?

4

NOVEMBER

Winter Is in the Air

A letter to the *Henley Standard*:

> Sirs:
>   The incessant noise from fireworks has distressed my
> llamas to the point where I have had to board them far
> outside the town limits. When will council act to restrict
> this appalling annual tradition?
> Sincerely yours,
> Gretchen Fawley-Smythe

I blame Guy Fawkes for the llama situation. A few years ago,
he objected so strongly to King James I and his policy of fining
Catholics for not attending the Anglican Church that he decided
to send the king back to Scotland by way of low orbit. On the
night before November 5, 1605, when the king and his cabinet
were set to meet, Fawkes and his accomplices snuck twenty barrels
of gunpowder into a rented cellar beneath Parliament. It was only
when one of the co-conspirators warned his brother-in-law not to
attend the meeting that they were discovered.

Fawkes was found guilty and executed opposite the Parliament
Building in January 1606 via the traditional method of drawing,
hanging, and quartering. This quaint custom began in the thirteenth century as a way of dealing with pirates, but proved to be
so popular with the general public that its use was extended to

high treason. Fawkes was dragged by horse to a square in front of Parliament and then strung up by a rope. Before he choked to death, however, he was cut down and his testicles and bowels removed. When he finally perished, his limbs and head were hewn off. The head was parboiled (keeps longer that way) and stuck on a pole especially reserved for the purpose on London Bridge.

Since then, Brits throughout the land have annually demonstrated their patriotism by removing various extremities of their own with high explosives. According to the Society for the Prevention of Accidents, more than thirteen hundred people are injured by fireworks every year. The largest single casualty group is male adults over twenty, with five-hundred-odd drunks and other unspecified dolts poking out eyes, setting their hair on fire, and one even sustaining anal burns (*ouch*). Amazingly, no one has been killed, which is a bit unfortunate when you think about the advantages this might have to the gene pool.

Henley's bonfire night is scheduled for Saturday, near the rugby grounds. The sponsors promise a visual extravaganza, with major fireworks lighting up the night skies and a huge Guy Fawkes roast over natural coals. Unfortunately, the day is marked with a massive downpour, and by the time the appointed hour rolls around, not even a gallon of petrol will ignite the effigy. Perhaps if they just parboiled him again, instead?

Fortunately, the rain lets up the following Thursday, just in time for Henley's open air market. It is a sunny day, but cool, and everyone out on the streets is dressed in thick sweaters, heavy coats, and warm mittens. I am walking down Reading Road toward Market Place when I meet up with Dave, the junior reporter at the *Henley Standard*. Dave is perhaps twenty-five, with a mop of curly black hair and a mischievous grin eternally fixed to his face. "Where you off to?" he inquires.

"I'm going to pick a few things up at the market."

"You'll love it, it's brilliant."

A man in an expensive leather coat walks past us on the sidewalk. A cellphone is clutched in one ring-bejewelled hand. He breaks off his conversation and turns abruptly to Dave. "Which way to the market?"

Dave, suddenly serious, respectfully points in the direction of Stoke Row. "Take the next left and go all the way to the top of the hill."

The man walks off without saying thank you. I wait until he is out of hearing range. "Why did you give him wrong directions?"

Dave's face breaks out in a grin again. "Well, it's a matter of civility, isn't it? If he had said, 'excuse me,' then I would have told him the right way to go."

"So, just because he was rude, you send him to Oxford?"

"Why not? It's an excellent school—maybe he'll learn some manners."

When I reach the Market Place, I am amazed to discover that the usual handful of stands that graces the weekly market has been augmented by at least a dozen large displays, complete with awnings. There are perhaps two hundred people crowded into the narrow aisles. I squeeze between aging women with their shopping trolleys and students from the college, the girls with bared belly buttons in spite of the cold, the boys in baggy skater jeans and thin denim jackets. Young mothers clog the narrow aisles with baby strollers, burying their infants under ever-increasing mounds of beans, honey jars, and Stilton cheese. An elderly man in a peaked woollen cap bites down into the hard, juicy pulp of an apple, his teeth popping out in the process.

As I wander up along the aisle, I can't help but notice that *organic* and *natural* are really big. The Acorn Herd Farm offers all things pork made from animals that are 100 per cent free of hormones, antibiotics, and bad vibes, having been raised in a primeval forest where they are free to snuffle about for tasty and nutritious acorns and old lager cans tossed from passing lorries. I must admit, the bacon does look happy; I buy half a kilo.

Nothing goes better with a rasher than a good fresh loaf. Flourpowercity, an organic baker, is selling a selection of soy bread, whole-meal baguettes, and free-range croissants. Two men dressed in aprons that state "Bread not Bombs" are behind the counter performing a Celtic song. One is beating out the rhythm on a large round loaf, while the other clatters two bread-cutting knives together and sings the lyrics.

I interrupt their gig to buy two whole-wheat carob brownies. They pop them into a recycled paper bag, along with a sample of their sun-dried apricot and walnut loaf. I continue on; Greensleeve apples, Devon lamb, oak-smoked trout, and beefsteak tomatoes from the Isle of Wight all tempt me, but I finally succumb to the pig roast. Two women in green and white checked aprons are presiding over a portable gas spit upon which a whole carcass has been mounted. Using a long carving knife, one woman hews slices of roasted meat into serving trays, while the other serves customers at a nearby table. "Will that be with crackling, stuffing, and apple sauce?"

I cheerfully agree to all three, and her assistant loads a fresh bun with a steaming helping of pork. "That'll be three quid, Love." I take my sandwich and find an empty spot on a nearby bench. The meat is moist and tasty and melts in my mouth. I can't say the same for the strip of crackling, however; I almost bust a molar biting into it. Fortunately a small pooch is more than happy to share it with me while her master is distracted at the pickled egg stall.

After I finish the pork sandwich, I join a long queue of shoppers waiting to buy cheese. The ambling pace of the line gives me an opportunity to cogitate upon Dave's theory on manners, and

I am busy writing notes when a grey-haired woman in sensible shoes provides a welcome distraction when she completely fails to notice the long line of shoppers and goes to the head of the line, picks up a slice of brie, and attempts to pay for it at the counter. The man in front of me, sporting a shaved head and the general air of someone who throws rocks for entertainment, speaks up: "*Oy*—we've been waiting for half an hour, and if we've done it, then it's only fair that *you* do, too."

The woman blushes furiously and beetles off with her wicker basket, painfully aware of her grave social error. Several tongues click "tut-tut" and there is the general shared conclusion that such a *faux pas* can only be punished by expulsion from the church auxiliary or perhaps a smart march around the square with her head on a pike.

You've got to love that about the British: such lovely civility mixed in with saucy irreverence and the occasional civil war. Cromwell would have approved.

Winter is definitely on the way. Each day is becoming cooler and shorter; at night the wind comes whistling down the valley from the north, and every morning the dew lies heavy on lawns and flower beds. It is almost 9 AM, and I am driving along Wargrave Road as I return to Henley after dropping Linda off at work. The rain, inexplicably, has held off for an hour, and the sun is just poking above the horizon.

As I approach the village of Wargrave, I pass a strawberry field on my left. The berries have long since been harvested, and the long lines of white plastic coverings that protect the roots meander across the black soil like languid anacondas, glistening with morning frost.

Traffic slows considerably as I enter the village. The High Street through the centre of town narrows to one lane near the

Bull pub, and I take my place in a long line of stationary traffic. The homes in Wargrave are mostly slate-roofed cottages, their façades covered in brilliant red Virginia creeper vine leaves. The light turns green and my line of cars slaloms through the centre of town.

Right at the edge of Wargrave, the road again widens. To the left is the marina, set in a back channel of the Thames. To the right is a wide expanse of lawn that sweeps up the hill to the steps of an immense white mansion; a herd of tiny, tame deer graze on the grass. Ahead is a dark tunnel of birch and chestnut, the branches arching over the winding road. As the rising sun touches the uppermost leaves, the canopy becomes a blaze of rustling gold.

None of which I appreciate at the time, of course. Sue, our rental agent, has managed to round up some oven cleaners, and I am in a rush to get back to Boathouse Reach before they arrive. I hit the road that winds some four miles between Wargrave and Henley, and push the gas pedal to the floor. As I accelerate, I keep a wary eye out for oncoming traffic, especially honey wagons. These are ten-tonne lorries mounted with steel tanks and piloted by Formula 1 drivers who think their cargo will go bad if they don't race as fast as possible to the sewage treatment plant.

The road is relatively quiet, so I turn my attention to scanning for wildlife. The surrounding forest is densely populated with badger, rabbit, and pheasant. As I round the corner near the turnoff for Crazies Hill (named for a type of buttercup that strews the fields hereabouts, or so the local schoolmarm tells me), I see the corpse of a small badger, perhaps two feet long, its tiny white face and black eyes covered in dried blood. It is, alas, a common sight; every year several thousand badgers, mostly young, are attracted out onto the asphalt to their doom by dead birds and other road pizza not agile enough to evade a fast-approaching car.

As sad as it is to see a dead badger, it is not altogether a bad thing. Red kites, once extinct in these parts, have recently been reintroduced into the Chilterns. The hawks are scavengers, and when the afternoon sun heats the dark earth, they soar far above the ground, searching for pulped critters to feast upon, badgers being especially tasty and nutritious. Unfortunately, various busybodies place butcher scraps out in their backyards in the mistaken assumption that trimmings are good for the birds. The problem, according to wildlife veterinarians, is that there isn't enough crushed bone and hair in butcher scraps to ensure that the red kites' eggs remain strong; the end result is that the eggs crack and the chicks die. One can't help but think these misguided morons would be doing the environment a true favour if they were to lie down on Wargrave Road and await the next honey wagon. Each one would be worth at least three badgers, and far less lamented.

When I reach home, a white van is parked outside. *Good As Nu Oven Cleaning* is emblazoned across the side, with the further admonishment, "Owned and operated in your community" printed beneath. Two independent franchisees, who appear to have recently escaped from Reading Gaol, are sitting on my front steps. Bonnie has bright red hair, black mascara, and a street corner grin; Clyde is small and stocky with a squashed nose, shaved head, and an invertebrate zoo tattooed on his massive forearms. I apologize for my tardiness and invite them in out of the cold.

While Bonnie applies a new layer of purple lipstick, her beau dismantles the oven using a small set of tools tucked into his waistband. Here's a man who knows his way around a kitchen appliance; within thirty seconds, he has removed the oven door and all the interior fittings. I get the distinct impression he could have disarmed my car alarm and removed the stereo, too.

Bonnie pauses in her toilette long enough to carry the door and fittings outside. Curious, I follow her to the van where she opens the back door. A large concrete vat is perched inside at the rear of the truck. Bonnie lifts the lid to reveal the steaming liquid inside.

"So, is Canada nice then?" she asks, as she plops the oven parts into the tub. I ignore her comment, distracted by a cloud of white gas rising from the noisily-bubbling fluid. "Is that acid?"

"Oh, heavens, no. It's lye."

Within the hour, the duo have thoroughly scrubbed the oven interior spotless and returned the loose bits from their bath. The job done, they hop back into the van and cheerily drive off. I wave as they depart; I can't help but think what a wonderful nation this is to kit out a former felon with a mobile lye bath, all in the name of commercial initiative.

I must say, I am beginning to warm to "wellies"—a.k.a. wellington boots. The epitome of rural sartorial expression comes in all colours, including pink for the ladies, yellow and blue for children, black for the biker crowd, and green for the farm lads. These utilitarian waders are worn shopping, hiking, and fishing, although their environment of choice is the barn. Tucking them inside the trousers is considered effete or, even worse, "continental," and never under any circumstances are the brims to be turned down. Children and Australians may don them with shorts, but nobody else.

I am standing in Woolworth's casually examining the boot display when Owen approaches. "*Oy*, got a little sheep shagging in mind then?"

"Shagging?"

"You know, *pulling*." Owen glances right and left along the aisle then mimics grabbing a small barnyard animal by the haunches and making a vigorous thrusting motion.

"*Oh*, I get it."

Owen shakes his head. "You Canadians are a thick lot."

I have to agree, especially when it comes to British words and phrases. "Naff," for instance, means out of date, but in a stupid way, like a cloth cap with a bright red pompom on the top. "Twee" is a similar word, only more effeminate, like putting lace curtains on your Ford Escort. "Nosh" is fast food, like "let's have a curry nosh then." "Posh" is classy, but not necessarily upper class. As in, "*Ooh*, that's a posh car." "Cosh" is what you do to someone's head with a lead pipe; "dosh" is a pile of loot, "mosh" is dancing with three hundred other people on a floor the size of a phone booth, and "tosh" is a load of crap.

I am thinking about all this tosh as I pass Chateau du Vin, situated on Reading Road opposite the post office. It is a restaurant and pub that is so inconspicuous that I would have missed it completely were it not for Richard waving energetically at me from inside as I walk by. I retrace my steps to the front door and enter.

The Chateau du Vin is perhaps six metres wide and thirty metres deep; the front is taken up by an ornate wooden bar and stools, the back part by a dozen or so dining tables. The room is dimly lit by sconces attached to the wood-panelled walls.

I join Richard and Dave at the bar, where they introduce me to a friend with whom they are drinking lunch. Terry is in his fifties, with a round, puckish face and a gut that bears witness to several decades of intense allegiance to beer.

I order an omelette from the lunch board then join the trio in a discussion of contemporary men's fashions. "Did you see that hairband that Beckham was wearing the other day?" says David. "What a prat."

Ah, more weird words. "What's a prat?"

"It's like a stupid fool," says Richard.

"Yeah, a real berk," adds David.

"Is a prat as bad as a twat?" I ask.

"No, a twat's worse," says Terry. "A prat isn't offensive, it's something you'd say to your mate to his face, like 'don't be such a silly prat.' You'd never call a mate a twat to his face; it's too rude."

"If you had to say someone was a prat, and someone was a twat, who would you say?"

"Hugh Grant is a prat," offers David.

"And David Prescott is a good example of a twat," says Terry.

"And the lot of you are English *merde*," says a voice from behind us and we are joined by the restaurant's owner. Claude is a tall man of mixed heritage, part East Asian and part French. He has the dour expression of someone who has committed too many indiscretions on his own part to have any lingering faith in humanity. He shakes my hand gravely then pours himself a glass of red wine and downs it in one large gulp. As an afterthought, he pours me a glass as well. "Do you enjoy wine?"

I humbly demur that, while my passion can't hold a candle to his, I do enjoy a good Burgundy now and again.

"Good. You must come to our Beaujolais Nouveau Day."

I am delighted to hear that Henley-on-Thames celebrates BN Day, and readily agree. This arcane annual ritual, held on the third Thursday of November, started more than fifty years ago in France as an opportunity for wine lovers to test the quality of Burgundy's most recent vintage. For those who think it's a shallow marketing ploy to get foreign rubes to guzzle overpriced plonk that nobody in France would feed to their dog, let me assure you that the good people of France do indeed feed it to their dogs, who on the whole drink and eat better than their children. While living in Paris in the early 2000s, Linda and I participated in several BN Days, and can wholeheartedly confirm that the French look forward to the event as much as Christmas.

My food arrives. The omelette is a fluffy confection of egg and cream wrapped around a filling of Gruyere cheese and French ham. "This is delicious," I exclaim. "Who's the chef?"

"Felix of Toulouse," says Richard. "He's brilliant."

At that moment, Felix emerges from the kitchen. He is a chubby man with a whisker-strewn face, wearing a white apron and plastic cooking sandals. He grabs Claude by the arm and gestures toward the door. "My wife, she calls. I must go—it is the plumbing." He motions a toilet overflowing.

Dave shakes his head as Felix departs. "A lot of the British think Henley is posh, but a lot of people in Henley are really struggling to get by. People who work in bars and shops can't afford to live here—they end up in hovels."

"You want to see hovels, you should try living in London," says Terry.

"You don't like London?" asks Claude. "But I am told it is the greatest English city in the world."

Terry shakes his head vehemently, "I'd never live there in a thousand years."

Ah, now there's a man after my own heart. I tilt my glass high. "Here's to one twat of a town."

The weather on Beaujolais Nouveau Day is cold and wet but clears up in the evening and the stars are shining brightly in the sky by the appointed hour. When we arrive at Chateau du Vin, Ricardo, a young Portuguese man with glistening black hair, is attending the bar. After pausing momentarily to admire his reflection, he greets us at the door, kisses Linda on both cheeks, and then escorts us to our table.

The international code established by the *Academie des Restaurants Française* stipulates that all French eating establishments be decorated with wicker chairs, wrought-iron tables, a framed photo of the Eiffel Tower, and slightly chipped Pernod ashtrays. One can tart things up with baskets of baguettes and such, but those four basics are required by law. As well as a menu, of course. No French restaurant is complete without *magret de canard*, *gigot d'agneau*, and *crème brûlée*. I glance down the *carte* and my mouth starts to water in anticipation.

We are invited up to the bar by Claude for the first tasting. Ricardo has uncorked three different brands and fills several glasses. From a purely technical point of view, Beaujolais Nouveau is not the most ideal way to test the vintage. First of all, it is fermented with special yeast that gives it undertones of banana, which is fine on a sundae but not so hot in red wine. It is also only two months old, so it still has many of the rough, acidic edges that take at least a year to dissolve. But when it has been an excellent year for growing wine in Burgundy, Beaujolais Nouveau is a bouquet of berries, a dance of divine indulgence on the tongue.

Too bad this isn't one of them. Ricardo discreetly spits his out into the sink.

"*Ugh*," pronounces Linda.

"It's not so *bad*," says Claude, who has purchased an entire pallet. "It kind of grows on you."

"So do plantar warts," I note. "You can always sell this as a topical cure."

Felix arrives with a tray of *hors d'oeuvres*. "What would you like for dinner tonight? I know—I shall make you my own *dégustation*!" He rushes off to the kitchen.

Some minutes later, Felix appears with the first plate. He has taken a handful of Nova Scotia scallops, seared them on the grill, and then served them in artichoke hearts with Hollandaise sauce. We inhale this down, mopping up the sauce with the basket of baguette so fresh it is still steamy. No sooner are we done than Felix returns with a platter of prawns. These are not the wimpy little shrimp that plague all restaurants with plastic placemats, but huge, lusty things that you split in half with a cleaver before frying in garlic and butter. We are given a slight reprieve when the next platter is a selection of Roquefort, chèvre, and brie with grapes and toast before Felix returns with our final course—homemade vanilla ice cream with nougat. Ricardo recommends we wash all this down with a *demi-sec* bottle of champagne from Epernay, which leaves us in the mood to sing several ditties in French.

Since Claude can no longer tempt anyone with the Beaujolais, he produces three bottles of English white wine that have been left by a vineyard rep for tasting. Although the bottles still have labels, it quickly devolves into a "blind tasting," as the wine seems to cause serious deterioration of sight after two sips. Fortunately, it also precipitates an impressive numbness in the mouth, so we quickly lose any sensation of taste. In fact, by the third bottle, we have unanimously decided that Titmouth-on-Wye, where the vineyard is located, ranks only next to St. Emilion as a nexus of the grape.

All too soon, this nectar has evaporated, and we reluctantly proffer a round of joyous salutations to the staff. My last clear memory of the evening is a vision of Felix swigging from a bottle of champagne and dancing with the sous chef in the kitchen.

I am assuming it is morning as I am afraid to open my eyelids, certain that daylight will cause my eyeballs to spontaneously explode. My mouth tastes as though I have been French kissing a weasel. My brain, when it functions, registers a large clamplike device attached around my forehead. I briefly entertain the notion of jumping out the bedroom window, but it's only a nine-metre drop and I might have to crawl up the stairs and throw myself out twice. Sigh.

I struggle downstairs where Linda has blessedly left some brewed coffee. I glance out the window and note that the wind is blowing so hard that the rain is falling almost horizontally. As a Canadian, I feel that I share a certain kinship with the British when it comes to the climate. Anyone who has ever lived in a place where a good day is one in which it snows less than a foot, where sleet is a harbinger of spring, and warm is any temperature above the point where your tongue no longer sticks to exposed metal, can appreciate the British approach to meteorology; it doesn't necessarily have to be nice at all, it just has to *improve*. Thus, if the wind drops from hurricane force nine to a level where slate shingles no longer scythe the air, then it is a fine time for a stroll.

In fact, over the course of a cup of coffee, the wind does indeed abate and the rain settles down to a soggy mist. Almost immediately, several people appear for their morning constitutional, dragging reluctant pooches on leashes. On the not-unreasonable grounds that this may be the finest it will get all day, perhaps for the week, I grab my raincoat and umbrella and head out for some fresh air.

Out on the river, a group of mature people are learning the basics of rowing. Their breath comes out in steam as they bend gamely over their oars, learning the correct way to scull. A flock of what looks like buzzards is observing their progress with avid interest.

"That there's a cormorant, Lad." I turn to greet George and his dog, Emma. I begin to suspect that the old man doesn't live in Maidenhead at all, but lurks behind a bush until he spots someone to talk at and then leaps out and ambushes them.

I can't think of anything particularly brilliant to say, and instead of doing the most logical thing—which would be to immediately run off at a fast clip—I fall back on that fail-safe rhetorical trick and simply repeat what I've just heard. "A cormorant?"

"Yes, indeed." George rubs his hands together at the prospect of giving a proper lecture to a captive audience. "You know, the Chinese take a baby cormorant from its mother's nest, put a ring around its neck, then train it to fish." He points his cane at the bird and makes a circling motion with the tip. "They send it to dive and grab a fish and come back to the dock, then they force the fish out of its throat." He nods to me. "They're quite clever, those Chinese fishermen."

Not half as clever, I imagine, as the Chinese chef who convinces someone to eat a carp covered in bird slobber. I am wondering how I can possibly extricate myself from George's clutches when Emma comes to my rescue. A swan, tempted by the potential for bread crumbs, has swum too close to the riverbank. Emma squares her sausage body over four tiny legs and launches herself, torpedo-like, into the water. Fortunately, Emma is far less deadly than a torpedo and the swan successfully escapes her attack with a throaty hiss and a graceful tack. George rushes to the edge of the water and issues a series of commands sternly ordering Emma back to shore—to which, given the frigid nature of the Thames, she readily complies—and George is able to fish her safely out of the water. While he is thus distracted, I make it my business to relocate.

About half a kilometre farther south, the Remenham Angling Society has a fishing allotment adjacent to the River & Rowing Museum. In spite of the weather, or perhaps because of it, ten men have plunked themselves down on the bank. They are all in their thirties to fifties, with thick winter parkas, large bellies rolling expansively over old blue jeans, and dirty sneakers. They have come equipped with an impressive array of catch nets, tackle boxes, and big umbrellas to ward off the rain.

I stop beside a man wearing a baseball hat that says "Joe's Maggot Shop" across the front. He has four rods that have been baited and propped on special poles. This is obviously strenuous work, as he has brought along a folding canvas chair in which to park his overexerted posterior. I stop and politely ask what he is angling to catch.

"Fish." He doesn't even turn in my direction, worried, no doubt that he might miss a telltale twitch in his fishing bob that would indicate the presence of prey.

"What kind of fish?"

"Whatever's in the river."

I am tempted to point out the various lures dangling from the branches above me and ask if flying fish also qualify, when he suddenly realizes what a surly berk he must sound like and adds, for my edification, "You know, bream, roach."

In the interest of full disclosure, I must confess at this point that I hate fishing. What other pastime requires you to spend thousands of pounds on sporting equipment for the pleasure of sitting in the rain for several hours in the futile hope that you might pull something named after a house pest out of an open sewer? These guys didn't even have a beer cooler, for Christ's sake. Joe Maggot pulls something out of the water. At first, I think it's a slug, but on closer examination it turns out to be a minnow, some two inches long. He pulls it off, tosses it into his creel, and then turns to me and triumphantly smiles; all I can think of are the words of that great *bon vivant* Samuel Johnson, who once observed, "A fishing rod is a stick with a hook at one end and a fool at the other."

I shouldn't be so hard on fishermen; after all, they have their own guardian angels. The Royal National Lifeboat Institution (or RNLI) is a charitable organization that has saved thousands of folks from a watery grave throughout the United Kingdom over the last 180 years. I know this because Derek is trying to sell me two tickets to their charity cruise on *The Hibernia* next Wednesday evening. "It's a right smart affair, everyone gets dressed up and it has live entertainment and a gourmet buffet," he enthuses.

"What's the point of an evening cruise in November?" I ask. "It'll be pitch black by 7 PM. You won't be able to see a thing."

Derek glances around, just to make sure he isn't being over-heard. "It's actually a bit of a surprise party for Andy. They're presenting him with a lifetime achievement award."

I'd love to attend, but I'm a bit squeamish at the thought of an eighty-tonne boat simultaneously hurtling along the Thames in the pitch black and serving Coronation chicken on toast. Derek is very persuasive, however, and I eventually give in. I just hope that they don't play any music from the *Titanic*.

The following Wednesday is cool and damp, and heavy clouds are hanging over the valley as we board. The ticket notes that dress is "smart casual," although, judging from the advanced age of the forty people on board, "oxygen mask" might be more appropriate attire.

The Hibernia is newer than *The New Orleans*, and although it is roughly of the same dimensions, it has a contemporary design. In the Caribbean, boats are glass-bottomed, but in Britain, they are glass-topped; the majority of the sleek top deck is enclosed in windows. As we set sail, a heavy shower starts to pound down, giving us an excellent view of the raindrops. Entertainment this evening is being supplied by Liverpool Len. Dressed in a black tux and sporting a permanently tan-wrinkled face, Len looks like a cross between Guy Lombardo and a raisin. He has come equipped with a boom box and half a dozen saxophones; as soon as he launches into his set of Lawrence Welk classics, I retreat aft.

The Hibernia has a covered stern deck where you can leisurely watch the world roll by. We head downstream, past the Hambleden Lock and into the stretch between Henley and Hurley, a rather bucolic area of weeping willows, otter dens, and caravan parks.

As smoking is not allowed in the main lounge, several pas-sengers have gathered on the rear deck to feed their addiction. The smell of Pall Malls mixes with perfume and the river's maritime odour in evocative fashion. If you lift your eyes up to the dark and forested shore, you can almost imagine yourself on a nineteenth-century barge wending its way through the countryside with a load of barley bound for London, its crew taking a pause from their daily labours to savour a pipeful of tobacco and compare cocktail dresses. One can only visualize shore leave.

Len finishes his set and the RNLI director summons everyone to the main room. Calling Andy to the front, he recites an impressive list of accomplishments, from organizing fun runs to supplying charity prizes and nautical support with his fleet of craft. Andy humbly accepts a plaque and a letter of commendation, and then it is time for the buffet.

The entrée for the evening is Coronation chicken, a concoction of cubed breast in a mild curry sauce (thankfully, without toast). I love to cook with curry; most people think of it as a relatively recent addition to the British take-away repertoire, but rumour has it Richard II introduced it to the isle back in the fourteenth century, along with the spoon, which he felt useful for eating soup. I fill my dish and sit down beside Andy's wife, Clare, who is attired in a lovely evening dress in coral silk. "You must be very proud of Andy," I say.

"The whole family is proud," she agrees. "He's done so very much." She turns toward Andy, who is busy explaining to the pilot the intricacies of nighttime navigation. "But he's going to be seventy soon. He should make time to enjoy the grandchildren, to travel, to have some fun. It's time for him to turn things over to the kids."

I agree with Clare and wish her the best of luck. Getting Andy to retire is going to be about as easy as removing a half-empty bottle of wine from a Frenchman's grip.

5

DECEMBER

The Festive Season

When the first of December arrives, Christmas decorations start to go up all over Henley. Along the main commercial streets, town workers are busy putting tiny evergreens into metal braces attached to the upper floor of storefronts. They are only about a metre tall and rather scruffy looking (the trees, not the workers), but I suppose it's the thought that counts.

We have invited Teddy over for dinner tonight, and when I stop at the butcher's to pick up some chicken breasts, I am informed by Mr. Trowbridge that the town council nicks each retailer £50 to participate in this particular stab at civic decoration. Personally, I think they'd be far better off spending the money on a swan roast for the poor.

As I walk past the Loch Fyne restaurant in Market Place, Moira, a young woman with raven-black hair, steps out of the front door and accosts me with a seductive Scottish burr. "Care to try my oysters?"

Tingles rush up and down my spine at the very thought. I picked up the habit of swallowing live bivalves in Paris. Gnarled and raspy, these gastronomic pearls rest in wooden boxes, each one chalked with its pedigree: Brittany, Normandy, the Bay of Biscayne. For around five quid, the fishmonger will shuck a dozen oysters then lay them on a bed of ice-cold kelp with a lemon on top. The only sensible thing to do then is rush right home and heap a tiny spot of red wine vinegar into each shell and slurp them down immediately. I glance over Moira's shoulder toward the display counter. "Are they fresh?"

She tosses her mane of hair. "Picked from the loch this very morning and rushed here by express train."

"Great. I'll have a dozen to go. Can you please shuck them?"

Moira's cheeks flush. "I can't sell them to you like that. They have to be eaten within ten minutes of opening."

"What if I bring my running shoes?"

"I'm sorry sir, it's the law."

I stalk out of the restaurant, muttering, "Bloody nanny state."

Richard is standing out front of Henley Town Hall within earshot. "And Merry Christmas to you too. What's got your goat?"

I explain the rules governing oysters. "I just can't believe all the stupid laws they have here to protect morons from killing themselves."

"Aren't they like that in Canada?"

"Are you kidding me? You can get drunk and run your Ski-Doo over Niagara Falls as long as you're wearing a safety helmet."

Richard is waiting to take a picture of the town mayor holding a ceremonial cheque for some local cause. He stamps his feet to relieve the cold and boredom. "What else is different between Canada and the UK?"

Several thoughts immediately spring to mind. Perhaps one of the biggest contrasts is that you are never truly alone in England. You can trek into the deepest bowels of the Chilterns and bend down and stare intently at some innocuous flower at the side of the trail. Invariably, after about thirty seconds, you will be joined by a pair of well-worn hiking boots. "That's a grub-billed bluebell—very rare," they will announce, worried that you might be thinking of despoiling the countryside by plucking and selling it to some Saudi billionaire.

In Canada, you have exactly the opposite problem. Let's say you're driving along the Trans-Canada Highway through

Northern Ontario. To the left is Lake Superior, a vast expanse of cobalt blue. To the right is coniferous forest, a wild and tangled carpet that runs unimpeded to the Arctic Circle. By now, the coffee from the Tim Hortons doughnut shop back in Nipigon has finally percolated its way through your lower intestines and yearns to be free. Pulling over, you step out of the car and walk for about thirty metres into the forest and step directly into a bear trap.

There you lie, in extreme pain and not a little embarrassment, wishing for once that a prospector might step out of the bush and say, "That's a fine example of a Busch & Stratton double-sprung grizzly-buster." Instead, your shrieks are far more likely to attract the attention of a bear, which will no doubt appreciate the *delicious* irony of the situation.

As for differences in cultural matters, I've noticed that Britain doesn't have "critics," they have "assassins with pens." I am especially fond of one A.A. Gill, the food critic for the *Sunday Times*. Any sane Canadian restaurant owner would rather have an outbreak of anthrax in her dining room than this man, but apparently UK restaurateurs are lining up to have their very expensive establishments eviscerated in extremely biting and witty epithets. Gill once observed that a certain restaurant's Kuala Lumpur chicken reminded him of the contents that spew from a Malaysian rat's maw when backed over by a lorry at low speed. Reviews just don't get better than that.

But the most interesting difference I have noticed, by far, is the unusual ways that British people have devised for killing themselves. A woman in Scotland recently offed herself with a dishwasher when she stumbled in the kitchen and fell upon an upturned knife. In a bid for one-upmanship, a Taunton man drowned while rescuing his cellphone from a sewer. He was on his way home from the pub when the handset fell onto the sidewalk and slid into a culvert. He lifted the steel grate and leaned into the drain, but lost his balance and fell in headfirst. A passing motorist saw his feet sticking out of the drain and pulled him out, but it was too late; he had already joined the Choir Celestial. Apart from a few imaginative dismemberments involving snowmobiles and barbed wire fences, Canadians can't hold a candle to this lot.

I explain all this to Richard, who nods in contemplation for a moment. "Would you like to do a piece on the topic for the *Standard*?" he says.

"I'd be honoured. Anything in particular I should mention?"

Richard glances up as the mayor finally makes his appearance. "Yeah. Don't include anything you just told me."

At lunch, Teddy calls and offers to take me on a tour of the country around Remenham, the village located just across the Thames from Henley. I walk over at about 3 PM; it is a crisp but sunny afternoon. The thick hedge that runs along the lane leading to his home at Barn Cottage has long since lost its leaves, and the low sun shines through its innards, exposing a rich selection of birds' nests hiding within its black, closely entwined branches. When I reach Teddy's home, he is standing outside on the back porch, warming himself in the sun. He points across the paddock where his horses once grazed. "See that house on the hill? The one with the large conservatory on the side?"

I turn toward the impressive mansion. "Yes, what about it?"

"My father used to own that."

"Who owns it now?"

"An ex-doctor." Teddy speaks out the side of his mouth, a habit of his whenever there is juicy gossip to impart. "Struck off the rolls, you know. Got caught selling internal organs for transplants. *Haw-haw.*"

Teddy has decided to buy me a pint at the Flower Pot, a pub located at the Aston ferry crossing, some five kilometres downstream.

He backs his car out of the garage. I think it is a Peugeot, but it is so old and decrepit that I cannot tell the make or model, as the badges appear to have rusted off. We set off at a blazing pace, I reckon around 11 kilometres per hour. As we trundle toward Aston along a narrow lane that has been cut into the hill above the adjacent river meadows, I notice that a section of the uphill side of the road is riddled with tunnels the size of dinner plates.

"Bloody badgers," explains Teddy. "They dig everything up. Half the road collapsed last year. You're not allowed to do beastly things to them, either. You have to wait until they leave before you can repair."

The Flower Pot is a tall, rambling building constructed of dark red brick. To one side, about three dozen chickens roam about in a large open coop, aimlessly pecking at the ground. We park in the lane and enter. The interior of the pub is decorated with angler's castoffs: the walls are chockablock with fishing rods, nets, and creels. Of special delight to Teddy is the collection of thirty-odd stuffed fish, each one mounted in a little glass-fronted case with a brass plaque detailing its length, weight, and where it was caught. "Do you like fishing?" I ask.

"Good Lord, no. Can't stand it. I do like fish and chips, though."

We order our pints and sit and muse by the roaring fire. Teddy points out the window. "I used to ride out here on my horse and take the ferry across to Hambleden. It was down at the end of the lane. A man had a raft attached to a line, and he'd pole you across the river for a few pence."

"When did they close the ferry?"

"1947." Teddy furrowed his brow for a moment, lost in a memory. "Seems like yesterday."

We finish our pints and return to town. By the time we reach Henley, Linda has the dinner well underway. She is preparing vodka penne, a delightful mixture of chicken breast, mushrooms, onions, and prosciutto ham prepared in a cream sauce then doused with vodka and flambéed. Over the course of the meal, Teddy consumes heroic amounts of Barolo and regales us with tales of all the girls he's kissed.

"There was this one lovely lady I met just after the war," he says. "Her name was Anne. I was with the RAF Transport Command, moving troops and government people around Europe, and I was supposed to fly her back from Rome. Well, there was no transport available, so we were stuck there for several days. What could I do but wine and dine her?" Teddy momentarily loses himself in reverie, until I call him back.

"Did you end up marrying her?"

"Heavens no! Stood me up, in the end."

"Too flighty?"

"Just the opposite—too much common sense."

The London Baroque Ensemble is performing its annual candlelit concert in St. Mary's Church this evening. Before that, however, I need to make a copy of a manuscript at Higg's Stationery Centre and get it in the post to a publisher in London. *Magnus the Magnificent* is an historical mystery novel set in the court of Henry V. Someone is trying to poison the king, and it is up to Magnus, the court jester, to unmask the villains. I have lost count of how many publishers have rejected it, but I take heart in the fact that James Joyce's *Dubliners* was given the thumbs down twenty-two times. This writing business isn't for the thin of skin, you know.

It is mid-December and, if anything, the weather is getting warmer. It's enough to give a Canadian the willies. I don a light jacket and head out the door. Most of the leaves have fallen off the trees by now, and I spot a big clump of mistletoe clinging parasitically to a tree at the corner of our parking lot.

Mistletoe is a droopy evergreen bush with spiky leaves and poisonous berries. Sounds like one sexy little shrub, doesn't it? The English developed the custom of puckering under this heinous bush in the belief that it would eventually lead to marriage. Funny it never occurred to them that brushing their teeth on a regular basis might be a better plan. As I head past, I give it a heartfelt whack with my umbrella.

The copy jockey at Higg's stands about five foot three and has slicked-back hair. When I hand him the manuscript, he sighs as though he is going to have to cancel his Christmas holidays this year. Nothing would please me more than to test to see if his pomade is flammable, but instead I amuse myself by examining the assortment of commercial Christmas cards displayed on the counter. They are a series of watercolours featuring festive winter scenes around Henley, with everything covered in a charming blanket of snow. My favourite card features a traveller in a classic Morgan sports car tooling his way across Henley Bridge toward the Angel pub. The ragtop has been retracted, the better to experience the bracing country air. I know it sounds silly, but I have seen this particular lunacy with my own eyes. For some reason that I have yet to fathom, the colder it gets, the more likely you will see sporty convertibles with their tops down tooling around Henley. Maybe it's because the drivers think they are less likely to suffer melanoma during winter solstice.

I post the manuscript and retrace my steps. As the sun sets, a cold breeze stirs up the valley. I am somewhat heartened until I arrive back home and discover Owen standing outdoors in his shirt sleeves using my driveway as an ashtray. "Do you think it will snow for Christmas?" I ask.

"It *never* snows anymore around here," he says. "Not since they put that big power station in upriver."

"What's that got to do with it?"

"They discharge the water into the river. It raises the temperature of the whole valley by five degrees every year."

I speculate that, at that rate, crocodiles will soon be taking over the wetlands around Mill Meadows, but Owen ignores me. "I swear, next year I'm taking my kids to Lapland for Christmas just so's I can point to the ground and say, 'There, *that's* snow.'"

In spite of Owen's prognostications, by the time Linda and I are ready to leave for the concert, there has been a distinct change in the weather and the evening has turned frosty; we dress in our finest coats and thick wool scarves before we depart. When we reach St. Mary's, a steady stream of people is already passing through the front portal.

This is the first time I have been inside the church, and I am surprised by its size and openness. The stone floor of the aisle that leads down the centre of the nave is worn by the shuffling of feet over the last five centuries. The transept, choir, and altar are enclosed by an intricately carved wooden screen. Several chapels sit in niches on the north wall, and the windows are richly adorned with stained glass depictions of Christ and the saints. The long wooden pews have been extended into the apse that follows the south wall, and there is sufficient seating for the four-hundred-odd audience that slowly files into the building. Wreaths have been hung on the pillars, and a side table has been set up to sell baked goods. The air is heavy with the smell of wool, candles, and almond cookies.

I have very fond childhood memories of going to the Anglican Church at Christmas. Every year, we would be dragooned into performing the Nativity procession on Christmas Eve, my brother Sydney and I working our way up through the progression of angels and shepherds until we were tall enough to fit into the splendid costumes of the Three Wise Men. Unfortunately, my religious pageant days came to an end when, along with Paul Cooper, Syd and I decided to embellish our roles as Melchior, Gaspar, and Balthazar by proudly whipping out cigars we had stolen from our dad's humidor and lighting them after the birth of the Baby Jesus. Reverend Creel subsequently banished us from the pageant and, if memory serves me correctly, from ever attending church on Christmas Eve again. People can be very intolerant of smokers.

Linda and I find a spot about ten rows back from the stage, which is set in front of the transept. Several pillows rest upon our pew, each one hand-embroidered with a biblical verse. One appropriately admonishes, "Thou shalt not covet thy neighbour's ass." We are barely settled when the concert begins. The electric lights are dimmed so that the honey-stone walls are illuminated solely by candelabra. The quartet enters and takes their places. Pachelbel's Canon in D floats through the church, the melody of violins soaring on the serene pulse of the cello. They are joined by a clarinet soloist, and the evening is rounded out with the Clarinet Quintet in A. This is one of Mozart's most sublime compositions, and the genius of his imagination is given full rein, the music climbing effortlessly into the highest realms.

After the concert, we head for home; the air is sharp and crisp after the warmth of the church. We scurry along the riverfront, our breath steaming from the cold, but before we reach the door to Boathouse Reach, I stop beneath the mistletoe and give Linda a warm kiss. Hey, I brushed my teeth.

Long before St. Mary's was built, or dental hygiene was invented, for that matter, there existed a river crossing near the present site of Hart Street. A member of the Reading Sub-Aqua Club was diving recently in the Thames approximately forty-five metres upstream from Henley Bridge when he discovered an ancient artifact. It turned out to be an iron sword in a bronze scabbard dating back two thousand years, which he donated to the River

& Rowing Museum, where it hangs on display. For something that's been sitting on the bottom of a river for two millennia, it doesn't look half bad; in fact, it looks almost exactly like something I saw yesterday while walking along the riverbank on the far side of the bridge.

Which explains why I am currently strolling along the shoreline peering intently into the shallow water. I would have liked to have dressed in traditional archaeological attire—leather jacket, fedora, and bullwhip—but they are, alas, back home in Canada. Instead, I have had to improvise with a baseball cap, white sneakers, and a high-tech grasping tool. It has a collapsible pole and a high-impact styrene clamping mechanism on the end. I suspect it might have been a walking cane with a folding seat in some former incarnation, but I have adapted it for scientific research.

The river bottom is littered with large objects, their origins obscured by thick fungal growth. Perfect. It looks exactly like every Jacques Cousteau documentary I've ever seen. Any moment now, I expect the little French elf to bob up from beneath the water and say, "*What secrets doo zee silent depths conceal?*"

I take out my notebook and record some observations. "Clarity of water: piss poor..."—*scratch that*—"...partially occluded by flocculants. Location of last sighting; approximately 100 metres to the north." I triangulate along the shore, deeply intent upon scanning the river bottom. As I pass, two girls eating sandwiches on a bench start to giggle. They wouldn't do that if I had one of those nifty rubber boats that Jacques and his gang used to skim along the coral reefs, *no siree*. Come to think of it, Jacques always used to stock his boat with bikinis, as well. I make a note to call Zodiac.

I am struck by the number of empty champagne bottles that litter the river bottom; was this the site of some ancient sybaritic rite, the likes of which would have boggled the imagination? Using my trusty grasping tool, I unearth a series of artifacts: Rayban sunglasses, lager cans, even a traffic cone. Leaving them on the shore for cataloguing by municipal employees, I continue on, zeroing in ever closer to my prey. There, just to the left of a duck, I spot it—the sword. It's encrusted with mud and algae and God knows what other crap, but I'm certain that there, just beyond my grasp, lies the weapon of an ancient Celtic king, dropped when the warrior was caught by a flash flood and drowned. I reach forward with my tool and gently grasp the scabbard, but as I lift it to the surface, it splits in two, one half of what looks suspiciously like a waterlogged stick floating back down to the riverbed, the other scooting off downstream in the current.

"Once again, zee elements of nature rise against man to conceal eet's secrets…"

It is the morning of Christmas Eve, and Linda is making butter cookies in the kitchen. I am out in the garage, rummaging around for a replacement vacuum bag when I come across a box of old *Times* newspapers left by the previous tenants. I pause for a moment, trying to decide what I'd rather do: vacuum the upstairs hallway or read a bin of six-month-old newspapers in a cold, ill-lit garage. Well, it's hardly a fair match, is it? I turn over a pail to sit upon and eagerly scan through the pile.

I am quickly rewarded with a curious tale of hot love gone bad. According to the story, a young Leicestershire man invited his fiancée for a romantic sojourn in a barn just outside of town. Lighting some candles for a romantic effect, they sipped champagne and made passionate love on the hay until they dropped into a deep slumber. Unfortunately, the candles lit the hay on fire; they awoke to find the barn ablaze and were only able to escape the conflagration by fleeing into the nearby field. When police arrived on the scene, they concluded that the naked couple were acting suspiciously and arrested the pair for arson.

I am interrupted by a summons from Linda. She is standing in the kitchen holding a small blender that we purchased in France. "I think it's broken."

"Here, let me have a look." I pry off the top of the food blender and examine it. Like everything else in this nanny state world, it has been designed with a safety catch so that some drooling imbecile doesn't take out his own eye. "Here's the problem—the safety catch doesn't click shut anymore."

Linda looks at it dubiously. "Maybe we should just get a new one."

"Nonsense." I fiddle with the lid for several seconds, experimenting with the mechanism. "There, that should do it." I clamp the lid back down and hit the *On* button, tilting it to one side. The lid falls off and the blades promptly leap out with the velocity of a v2 rocket. They clip the face of the fridge and then proceed to buzz around the kitchen as Linda and I dive for cover. By the time it is all over, the blades have chiselled impressive gouges out of several cupboard doors, but other than some stains in my underwear, I am unscathed.

Not only that, but apparently I've solved the problem of what to get Linda for Christmas; she has decided she wants a new husband. Ha-ha. I retreat to Chateau du Vin for a glass of Yuletide ale with Richard and David. "Any ideas what gifts you'll be getting this year?" I ask.

"I'm hoping my Jan will buy me a guitar," says Richard.

"Do you play?"

"No."

I scratch my head. "Then why do you want Jan to buy you a guitar?"

"I just think it would be a nice thing to do." It turns out Richard has spent the last few weeks mooning and sighing over various guitar magazines that David has lent him. "She hasn't got the hint yet."

I suggest he replace the guitar magazines with a banjo publication. "She'll buy you a guitar just to keep her own sanity."

"Actually, I'd fancy a banjo too," says Richard.

David peers at me over the top of his Coke. "Do you know the difference between a banjo and an onion?"

"No."

"Nobody cries when you cut a banjo in half."

Richard ignores us, lost in thought. "I could get a job playing at funerals and such."

I glance at my watch. "Well, if you truly expect to get a guitar for Christmas, you're going to have to break down and tell her."

Richard looks at me, askance. "I'd never do that!"

"Why not?"

"It's just *not done*."

After several toasts to the season, I leave Richard and David and head for the ironmongers on Duke Street. I don't know why more people don't Christmas shop at the hardware store; they have such a wide selection of attractive yet practical gifts. Mother loves gardening, so I get her a small chainsaw. My brother Syd enjoys the outdoors, so I buy him an inflatable life raft and a collapsible plastic paddle. My niece Aletta, age six, gets a magic wand that can also double as a fly swatter.

The hardware store is almost deserted, so I spend a leisurely hour wandering the aisles. In addition to a new food processor, I spot several stocking stuffers that I just know Linda will be delighted with, including an electric pepper grinder shaped like Venus de Milo.

I make my purchases and continue on to Waitrose. Glancing through the supermarket window, I see that it is chock full of people doing last-minute shopping for gift packages. In Henley, "gift packages" usually take the form of a basket lined with shredded green polyethylene in order to resemble a chicken's nest—nothing wrong with that, especially if you keep poultry as pets, but it is then filled up with what can only be described in the most generic sense as "food." Linda, for instance, was given one by Cornelia, her boss. It contains a jar of rhubarb marmalade, a box of shrimp crackers, four bags of lemon grass tea, a half-bottle of elderberry wine, a lump of fruitcake, and a tin of Norwegian salmon. The hamper is wrapped in crinkly plastic that sparkles with an iridescent oily sheen. The only thing remotely edible is the tin of salmon, which bears a "best before" date of 2164. There's something reassuring about a tin of salmon that's good for a century and a half; no doubt the Franklin Expedition could have used a case or two. I figure I can find something equally as endearing for Cornelia, perhaps a bag of frozen turnips.

As I approach the supermarket's front door, I am sidetracked by a rather inebriated version of "We Three *Kinks*." Dale the busker is sitting on an upturned milk crate in the passageway that leads from Bell Street to the Waitrose parking lot. He is wearing a Santa hat tilted jauntily to one side and strumming on his guitar. I dig 50p out of my pocket and throw it into his open guitar case. He smiles and thanks me, then launches into "Rudolph the Red-*Necked* Reindeer."

Dale is, without a doubt, the most laid-back person in Henley. He wears blue jeans, old sneakers, and a tattered hand-knit sweater, and lives in an RV parked by the rugby club on the edge of town. His pale blue eyes and curly, sandy-coloured hair give him a boyish appearance that no amount of cheap rum will ever fade.

"How's the busking?" I ask.

"Not the best."

"I thought it would be good this time of year, what with all the millionaires in town."

Dale takes a swig from a bottle he keeps tucked beside the crate. "How do you think they got that way? Short arms and deep pockets."

"You planning anything special for Christmas?"

"Yeah, I'm going to visit me mum in Oxford."

"How about your Dad?"

Dale smiles ruefully. "My dad was a US serviceman at the military base north of Oxford. Mum met him briefly at a bar when she was seventeen."

"Doesn't she even know his name?"

Dale shrugs. "I don't know. We've never talked about it, Mum and I."

"Why not?"

"'Cause we're English." Dale takes another swig of his bottle and continues his set.

Waitrose is out of frozen turnips, but I find a wonderful sampler collection of barbecue seasonings with a label featuring a donkey with fire coming out of its butt; Cornelia will love it. It is quite dark when I leave the shop. I have purchased some eggnog for Dale, but he is nowhere to be seen. I place the jug beside his vacated milk carton and silently wish him a safe journey to Oxford.

Christmas morning in Henley dawns cold and blustery, a far cry from our first traditional English Christmas a few years back, which actually took place in the Canary Islands. That year, we had decided to forego Christmas in South Kensington in favour of celebrating in a warmer and friendlier climate. We had settled on the town of Porto Blanco on the main island of the Spanish colony off the African coast as a surefire bet. Little did we know we were flying into excursion holiday hell.

Our first hint that we had committed a dire mistake occurred when we glimpsed our accommodations: the Trés Estrellas. The mattress in the bedroom looked as though it had been purchased at a crime scene. The interior of the kitchen microwave was encrusted with what looked like the remains of red and green

Gummy Bears and the patio planter boxes had been used as ash-trays by the Lancashire Lung Cancer team. We took one look, dropped our bags, and fled into town.

Once upon a time, the seaside town of Porto Blanco must have been a quiet, charming place, its original outline barely visible in the steep, sloping valley that rose from a pretty, crescent-shaped beach. That was before the onset of cheap flights from Birmingham, however. Since then, most of it had been obliterated by inflatable toy shops, bikini-wax clinics, and bingo beer halls. The restaurants featured a wide assortment of spaghetti with Spam and chips, all swilled down with pints of effluent in the form of chilled lager.

That's not to say everyone wasn't having fun. The favourite attraction seemed to be the tattoo parlour. The clientele were lined up out the door, eager to add to their already impressive collections of demons, reptiles, and girlfriends named Liz. One man from Liverpool had shaved his head bald just to create sufficient landscape to add a coil of rattlesnakes to his collection.

We thought the Trés Estrellas couldn't get any worse, but we hadn't counted on the Christmas Day buffet. The staff decided to do a "Traditional English Meal" of mashed potatoes, mashed peas, and mashed turkey. I had always thought I would have to be sentenced to solitary confinement for dismembering a minor to deserve a holiday meal like this, but apparently even the serial killers in Wormwood Scrubs don't suffer the indignity of eating a bird that has been mechanically stripped from its bones and refashioned into a Tootsie Roll. And in a touch worthy of Stalin, they randomly included unshelled walnuts. After one bite, I retreated to the dessert buffet and helped myself to half a dozen dollops of lime-green pudding, hoping that they hadn't hidden any marbles in it.

In contrast, Christmas Day in Henley-on-Thames is relatively subdued. The tattoo parlours are all closed in observance of the holiday, and the only raucous action is the pealing of bells from St. Mary's tower. Linda and I arise and descend to the living room. Our tree is a three-foot-tall specimen purchased from the flower girls who set up a stall in Market Place. The tree is decorated in red and blue baubles and a string of electric lights. The lights, made in Taiwan, have a programmable switch that allows you to choose from a wide selection of flashing displays, from *twinkledash* to *lovebaby*.

Linda sits down to open her presents; she has been hinting at something with diamonds in it and is particularly impressed by the glass-cutter (at the very least, she is struck speechless). I am delighted to discover that Santa has left a chocolate orange in my stocking. This is a baseball-sized candy that splits into twenty slices when you tap it on one end. I rap it on the coffee table a little too enthusiastically, however, and shatter the glass covering. Linda is a little annoyed until I point out my foresight in getting her a glass-cutter. She suggests that a rolling pin might have been more to her liking.

After coffee, I place the turkey in the oven and we head out for a walk in Mill Meadows. Located adjacent to the Thames, just south of Henley, Mill Meadows is a wide, grass-covered field that has been purposely left largely undeveloped due to its tendency to flood during storms. According to the *Henley Standard*, teenagers also find it an excellent venue to drink tinned ale and moon one another.

It is a grey day with a fine mist falling, but the path is fairly crowded with pedestrians. Town folk nod gravely to us and murmur "Merry Christmas," as though saying it out loud to strangers is a bit risqué. A golden Lab, unmindful of the solemn day, races gleefully in and out of puddles, the resultant jets of spray tinkling in the air.

We take the horse bridge that carries us toward Marsh Lock. Water is flooding through the adjacent lock at full throttle, the roar echoing up and down the nearby hills. A man in a dark blue sweater with leather shoulder patches is standing at the entrance to the lockkeeper's booth, talking on the phone. Arthur is an employee of the Environmental Agency, the government body that controls the river levels. He glances at me warily as I approach but is friendly enough when I introduce myself as a newcomer to Henley.

"I thought you might be one of the homeowners," he explains, pointing to the high water above the weir. "Every time the water rises, I get blamed, as if *I* had anything to do with them building on a flood plain." He points to a large brick home that sits on the bank immediately below the weir. "Her home will be the first to get flooded—it just pours through the front door into her dining room."

The phone rings and Arthur goes off to answer it. I can hear the caller's angry voice, even above the roar of the weir. I hope someone bought the poor woman an inflatable life raft for Christmas. Lucky thing the ironmonger has them on sale.

We return home. The house is filled with the warmth of the oven and smell of the turkey. We mix a pitcher of rum and eggnog and retreat to the upstairs lounge. I set the Christmas tree lights to *jamjam* and we settle into the sofa, wishing our family and friends, wherever they may be, a Merry Christmas.

Our big plan for New Year's Eve is to find some lobster to barbecue. You'd think that an island nation would have a good handle on seafood, but the closest thing I've been able to locate is breaded crab balls in the frozen food section, which sounds about as appetizing as Rocky Mountain oysters.

In fact, I'm so put off that I decide to chuck the maritime theme completely and make it one big Italian night. I settle for Florentine delight, a rib steak done in a glaze made from rosemary,

HP sauce, mustard, and garlic, then barbecued to a medium rare. I serve it with baby potatoes and a salad made of rocket leaf, Parma ham, and shaved Parmesan cheese. A wonderful bottle of Barolo rounds out the meal.

We are just finishing dinner when the fireworks start. There is no formal display, merely the predilection that local citizens have for mixing alcohol and high explosives in large quantities. Since Guy Fawkes Day, there has been no let-up in angry letters to the *Henley Standard* regarding their effect on small furry creatures. You'd think that, with all the thatched roofs and whatnot around, one might also argue for their elimination on safety grounds, but apparently the accidental torching of an orphanage or two is incidental to animal rights activists. Adrian, our young neighbour a few houses down, has invited a few friends over in order to hurl empty champagne bottles into the river and fire Roman candles off his balcony.

Midnight arrives; we toast the New Year and head for bed. But not, it seems, for sleep. I am about to retire for the night when the flashing light of an emergency vehicle catches my attention. Worried that something might be amiss at the marina, I don my coat and head around the corner. I am relieved to discover that nothing has happened to the boats; the flashing lights are from an ambulance. I approach an idle attendant and ask what has happened; he explains that two drunks have plunged out the third-storey window in an adjacent apartment building while blowing on toy whistles. Fortunately, their fall was broken by a heap of patio furniture and they only suffered a few broken bones. I wish the attendant a Happy New Year and head back home. Perhaps, with any luck, furniture diving will catch on. I must mention it to Adrian.

6

JANUARY

The Flood

We wake up on New Year's Day to discover the river has risen above its banks and crept across the marina. A foot of water laps against the base of our house, much to the amusement of the ducks. I don some rainclothes and go round for a closer look. Derek is wandering about in his waders, peering through the window of a Jaguar convertible that is parked amidst the river's new bed. Already, a shiny slick of petrol is snaking its way out from the rear of the car and coiling around a trio of swans that paddle around the backwater.

"The owner's in New York for the holidays," he explains. "We're trying to find a set of keys."

"What happens if you don't find them in time?"

Derek smiles. "Not to worry—we'll muddle through somehow."

Of course. Persevering in the face of adversity and all that. Mind you, it's fairly easy to keep a stiff upper lip when it's someone else's Jag.

Owen shows up and lights a cigarette. We stand and contemplate the water as it rises slowly to the bottom of the Jag's doors. "This reminds me of the time my car ended up in the lake," he says.

I'm almost afraid to ask. "How did it do that?"

"Forgot to set the parking brake. Had to get a tow truck to pull it out."

"Did it still run?"

"Yeah, but the insurance company wrote it completely off anyway. They told me, what with the computer and electronics, I would never have anything but problems with it."

I watch the water lap against the Jag. "I'd hate to have that happen to my car."

"Then you'd better take care."

"What do you mean?"

Owen points to the side of our house, where the water has advanced up an alleyway to the front. "This water comes up any higher, you'll be floating away, too."

After that, I find myself nervously checking the level every quarter hour. It's not that I can't swim, it's just that I've never done it while clutching a twenty-eight- inch TV above my head. I know it's women and children to the lifeboats first when abandoning ship, but what's the protocol for a townhouse? And how exactly do you go about requesting a lifeboat for a building? I've seen those pictures on the news where people are being helped off their roof by rescuers in a rowboat, but have you ever noticed a phone number on the side?

Right, it's time for action; I get in the car and go to buy some wellies. By the time I get to Woolworth's, however, the shelves have been completely cleaned off. "Best try Wyevale's on Reading Road," the clerk informs me.

If, by some misfortune, you die and end up in Englishman's Heaven, then I suspect it will look very much like Wyevale Garden Centre. Masses of red and white cyclamen, bags of potting soil, and endless bird baths are stacked adjacent to books on the Second World War, display cases for fireworks, and a special section of lap trays for eating dinner while watching footie on TV. It has an essence of peacefulness and leisure about it that hangs in the air, full, ripe, and loungeful. All that's missing is free lager.

Thankfully, Wyevale's hasn't been cleaned out, and I find a fine pair of green rubber footwear. By the time I return to our house, however, the rain has let up and the clouds have parted. In defiance of the annoyingly sunny weather, I don my new boots and head out for a good wade down Station Road. Or, that's the intention. I arrive at the corner adjacent to the river to discover that the water has reached a satisfactorily deep level for a good splash, but it seems that the town's sewage system has also contributed to the festivities in the form of paper streamers and little brown *hors d'oeuvres*. I find this sort of thing tends to take the fun out of a good splash, and head, instead, for Mill Meadows, where the advancing waters have allowed the swans to paddle all the way to the parking lot where they are in the process of helping themselves to all the cigarette butts floating about. Ah, nature at its finest.

By the time I return to Boathouse Reach, the smell of dinner fills the house. We have decided to cook a traditional British meal for New Year's Day—roast beef. The recipe calls for a rib roast, seasoned with bacon lard and salt and pepper, seared, then set into a roasting pan along with potatoes, carrots, and onion. The secret, of course, is to withdraw it from the oven while the centre is still pink, then allow the juices to cook it to perfection. Thick, artery-clogging gravy, prepared with red wine and just a hint of horseradish, is obligatory. We make a resolution to eat just as well for the next three hundred and sixty-four days, if we live that long.

Although it has stopped raining by the time we finish supper, the water continues to rise, creeping ever higher on the flanks of the Jag. Around 10 PM, however, a large yellow tow truck with a flashing yellow light arrives and backs its way through a foot of filthy water. A man in knee-high waders steps out of the cab, his beer gut hanging over a pair of blue rugby shorts. He surveys the aquatic mess then unloads a steel dolly. By touch, he assembles the complex mechanism under the rear axle and then attaches it to his lift. He hoists the rear of the car into the air and tows it safely to solid ground, where he unhooks the vehicle and drives away. In a way, I am sad; I had a vision of the Jaguar floating leisurely down the Thames, through London, and out into the North Sea where its owner would eventually spot it as he flew back from America. It strikes me as a particularly charming way to end a holiday.

The next morning, I head down to the kitchen, half-expecting to see our coffee machine bobbing about, but I am greeted by a mercifully dry carpet. Overnight, the river has dropped about a foot. The ice that formed on the previous evening now clings like thin, translucent collars of glass around the light poles and steel bollards that line the river's edge. The ducks and geese that were formerly cruising past the base of my balcony are now waddling through an inch of mud, nuzzling beneath its surface for whatever nibbles might be concealed there.

The hour arrives for Linda to head for work in Reading. Unfortunately, Wargrave Road still remains partially underwater and impassable for anything short of an amphibious assault vehicle or hovercraft, neither of which came with the furnishings. Likewise, the Sonning Bridge across the Thames is only negotiable with a snorkel. Glancing at the map, I note that a series of country lanes skirt Wargrave Road along higher ground. Deciding that it was as good a day as any to see the countryside, we set out on a voyage of discovery.

Traffic is relatively light, perhaps because everyone else already knows the futility of travel this day. We cross Henley Bridge and climb White Hill unimpeded. About a mile past the crest, we come to the old turnpike road running east toward London. Turning right, we trace a crooked trajectory through field and pasture.

There is something about a narrow English country lane that causes a deep emotion to rise within me, and that emotion is terror. The engineers who decided to pave the tiny lanes running between steep impenetrable hedgerows, and then populate them with steel-bumpered Range Rovers, are sick, sadistic bastards. I get no farther than one hundred metres down the road when a tractor pulling a wagon full of hay appears in the opposite direction. By cleverly subjecting the side of my car to a thorn-bush scrub, I manage to squeeze by, only to have a city stockbroker in a Mercedes overtake me while dialing his cellphone.

Mind you, the view isn't bad. In between bouts with the flora and demented local drivers, we wind our way through several charming little villages. Thatched-roof cottages, shaggy-haired ponies in tiny paddocks, and oak-beamed barns nestle by the side of the lane. Had my fright abated sufficiently to take my eyes off the road for more than ten milliseconds, I dare say I might have enjoyed the tour. As it is, when we finally emerge on the dry side of Wargrave, I am filled with the kind of elated vigour that only a successful brush with death can imbue.

Once we are outside of the Thames Valley, traffic proceeds as if the flooding had never occurred. By the time we return that evening, the water has receded from Wargrave Road, allowing us to poke slowly home through the puddles of ooze left behind. We are, like everyone else on this isle, learning to muddle through.

I am scanning the *Times* for a summation of the flood, but it has been five whole days, and by now its place has been taken by more pressing news, to whit, the naked rambler. A man walking the length of Britain in the buff has once again been arrested. Stephen, age forty-four, started off from Land's End in southwest England in June wearing nothing but socks, shoes, a hat, and a backpack. His intended destination is John o'Groats, 1365 kilometres to the north on the far tip of Scotland. The former British Royal Marine had expected to walk an average of thirty-two kilometres a day and finish the journey within six weeks, but numerous arrest charges for breaching the peace and two jail terms have extended his odyssey by six months.

For those of you who have never lived in the UK, the "eccentric Englishman" has a certain apocryphal ring to it, like alligators in the sewers of New York. But spend a fortnight on this blessed isle and you will discover that idiosyncrasy is not only real, it is thriving. It's been a few months since I last caught sight of Colonel Bogey, but earlier this morning I spotted an interesting new specimen at a petrol station. As I stood by the magazine rack, a small red car pulled up and a man disembarked from the passenger side. He was wearing red plaid pajamas and a pair of moccasin slippers with little beading and fur-trim decorations. His hair looked like it had been styled with axle grease. He picked up a pint of chocolate milk and a pack of fags; just as he was paying for his purchases, however, his girlfriend decided to drive off and leave him stranded. Unperturbed, he set off down Reading Road chugging his choco milk and puffing on a Carlton Light.

Henley, of course, has its own variation on eccentricity: *Thamesitis*. In its mildest form, it causes the mildly delusional to waste huge amounts of money on a succession of floating gin palaces. In its more advanced stages, sufferers don latex clothing and paddle about in competitive fashion. And, in the most severe cases, victims abandon the firmament completely and become what is known in the psychiatric world as "barge nuts."

I am roused from my perusal of the paper by the front doorbell. When I open the door, Derek is standing there with a man holding a bucket and an extension pole. "This is Steve," he explains. "He's here to do the outside windows. Can he come in?"

I've always assumed it's a lot easier to clean the outside of a window from, well, the outside, but hey, I'm not one to argue with a professional doing his job, so I stand to one side and let the man in. Climbing the stairs to our second floor, Steve lets himself out onto the balcony where he can do both the patio doors and the upstairs windows overlooking the river. "I don't like using ladders," he admits as he screws his extension pole together and begins to lather the top windows. "I'm afraid of falling off."

This strikes me as a bit of a deterrent to a career in window washing, but Steve, it turns out, is really a mooring bailiff who does windows on the side during the off-season. Steve explains that mooring bailiffs are the local officials in charge of going up and down the river collecting the daily rent from boats that have docked by the shore for the evening. This is a big gig around these parts, and Steve tells me that fees can reach £25 day during the regatta.

With the upper windows finished, Steve relaxes a bit and reveals that he lives with his wife in a "narrow boat," a steel-hulled barge that has been equipped with living quarters. Since many of the waterways that criss-cross the UK are only seven feet wide, narrow boats are built with a maximum beam of six feet ten inches, allowing a comfortable clearance of one inch on either side.

I've never been in a narrow boat, and I ask for a tour. Steve is more than happy to invite me for a visit and, after he has finished the windows, we take a tiny fibreglass tender boat to Cottage Eyot, an island in the Thames just upstream from the River & Rowing Museum.

The *Putney Princess* is about fifteen metres long, its steel hull painted green, and the superstructure decorated a sprightly red with traditional gold filigree swirls. We enter through a pair of aft wooden doors and step down into the main cabin. The steel hull is still partially exposed on the inside; the boat has only been in the water a few months, and Steve is still installing the "noggings," the wood frame used to attach the interior fittings. Still, enough of the inside has been finished to live comfortably, if your idea of comfortable is an escape tunnel under Stalag 17.

"The first thing that people think is that it must be damp inside, but it's not," says Steve. I have to agree—claustrophobic, maybe, but definitely not damp. I ask what he really loves about his home.

"Owning a barge is like having a floating home," he replies. "When you go somewhere, you can literally take the kitchen sink with you." I squeeze into a tiny nook as he pops the kettle on a propane stove and brews up a cuppa for afternoon tea. A swan taps its beak on a porthole and begs a biscuit. Steve opens the round window and passes one out. The swan takes it and paddles off, Steve watching as it disappears downstream. "I guess I like the sense of freedom most."

After tea, Steve rows me back to the mainland. On the way home, I notice that a man is sitting on a folding picnic chair in the middle of the meadow. He is perhaps fifty years old and dressed in a heavy coat and a bright pink woollen scarf. He is puffing on a pipe and reading his newspaper, which whips about in the cold arctic air blowing across the open field. As I pass, he looks up and nods amiably. I nod back, comforted in the knowledge that there will always be room in England for the deranged.

By the time mid-January arrives, I have finished writing my column for the *Henley Standard* and filed it with Richard. The following day, he calls me on the phone. "I need to take your photo. Do you have any Canadian clothing you can wear?"

"You mean like hockey pads or a lumberjack shirt?"

"Yeah."

"Sorry, I left them behind with my snowshoes." All I have is a well-worn T-shirt with a maple leaf flag that I wear when running.

Richard sighs. "I guess that'll have to do. Meet me at the bridge at noon."

Richard arrives at the appointed hour carrying a large black digital Nikon camera around his neck. "Let's get some pictures of you first, then I'll buy you a pint at the Angel and we can talk."

At the far end of the bridge is a sign welcoming visitors to Henley and informing them that the town is twinned with Falaise, France. Richard positions me adjacent to the sign, then shoos off a passerby who has draped his arm over my shoulder. After heartily cursing the controls for several seconds, he eventually takes my picture.

When we are done with the sign, Richard leads me back across the bridge to St. Mary's. The cathedral's tower is a rather impressive affair, built of honey-coloured limestone and inlaid chert nodules and rising some thirty metres in the air. The top above the belfry is flat and square, with crenellations like a fort and four tiny hexagonal towers marking the corners. If the Tower of London were made of taffy and you gave it a pull, the outcome would look not unlike the structure behind me now.

I offer to climb to the top of the tower and wave down, but Richard declines. "It's a bit of a climb, I assure you." Apparently, there is a dark, narrow, circular stair followed by a rickety stepladder ascent through a trap door, which thrills me about as much as rappelling up the side. We opt instead for a few snaps at sidewalk level while an old man whistles from a nearby window and compliments the pretty Canadian boy.

The third pose is by an almost-authentic British phone booth sitting in Henley's Market Place. I say almost, because although it is red and has the old-fashioned swinging wooden door, it lacks the lively selection of business card–sized advertisements for women of "easy leisure" that are commonly found in the phone booths of London. I use the term "women" loosely here, because they are, by a vast majority, *he-girls*. These ads offer a variety of services and are accompanied by photos of leather-clad models with pierced nipples.

I understand that schoolboys have made a hobby of collecting them, swapping with their chums to complete the entire set. "I'll give you two S&M Sallies for Olga the Dominatrix."

"Throw in two fags and you've got a deal, mate."

I'm sure Mum is relieved when all she finds in her son's back-pack is a deck of large-breasted hookers with tool kits and not crack cocaine.

"Okay, that's it," announces Richard. "Let's get some lunch."

Lunch in Britain consists of what Canadians generally refer to as a "barley sandwich." While the Angel barmaid is pouring our main course, Richard asks how my book is coming along.

"Great. I need something more about this flood, though."

"You should check out Shiplake," says Richard. "They got it a lot worse than us."

Later that week, I set off on an expedition to the town south of Henley. Shiplake has neither ships nor a lake; its name harkens back to the pits that medieval shepherds would dip their sheep in before harvesting the wool. It sits about five kilometres upstream from Henley, just east of Toker's Green (nobody has any idea of where that name came from). Since it is a cold, rainy day, I decide to forgo the *Henley Bullet*, the spur train that runs through Shiplake on its way to the mainline at Twyford, and walk along the river towpath.

My plan is less lunatic than it sounds, or at least, that's what I tell myself. I have decided that, in the spirit of cultural immersion, I will emulate that most iconic symbol of English eccentricity, the Rambler. These hearty folk, denizens of the nation's cities, set off each weekend in anoraks, thick brown woollen scarves, and sensible shoes with the express purpose of enjoying nature throughout the realm. And woe unto any country squire who places a barrier in their way, for they shall march right over their garden patch in righteous indignation and poke the offender with their pointy walking sticks in the name of good neighbourliness. You gotta love this country.

I encounter no country squire on my way to Marsh Lock, which is just as well, as I have little appetite for poking anyone with a stick this morning. Instead, as I slog through a meadow that has been churned to muck by scavenging cattle, I meet a man heading in the opposite direction. Mike is in his mid-forties, with a balding head, mud-stained dungarees, and a complexion made florid by several decades of cider. He is, at the moment, clutching a two-litre plastic jug of said beverage, now largely evaporated. We stop to chat, and I ask his destination.

"The graveyard," he states in slightly bleary fashion. I consider this a rather philosophical reply until he explains that the tiny patch adjacent to St. Mary's Church in central Henley is an excellent place for a quiet nap before continuing on to his ultimate destination, which is Wargrave. Mike, it turns out, is a pilot for a Middle Eastern airline and, to prevent dehydration in that arid clime, he spends as much time as possible on his off-days walking about in the rain and absorbing fluids.

"And where are you going?" he asks.

"I thought I'd explore Shiplake."

"Ah. Bunch of rich snotholes. Damn good pub, though. Remember to stop at the Baskerville Arms."

I thank Mike for his suggestion and continue my slog until I come to Shiplake. The town itself is the kind of perfectly manicured village that gives you the feeling you are being watched from behind lace curtains. The grand homes are situated well back from the lane, many surrounded by high fences and marked by security alarm banners. There is no High Street, but the eleventh-century

Norman church is so well preserved that I half expect William the Conqueror himself to sic a bull mastiff on me as I wander through the graveyard fruitlessly searching for monkshood, traditionally the first blossoms to appear in January.

Noon is approaching, and so I forgo wandering about in the rain and retreat to Shiplake's one and only pub, the Baskerville Arms.

Pub grub in England has undergone a lamentable sea change in the last few years, with gorgonzola cheese melts, Vietnamese sausage wraps, and *foie gras* tortillas replacing the traditional artery-clogging fare. Thankfully, the Baskerville Arms' menu is leavened with a filling assortment of sausage-and-mash, fish 'n' chips, and steak and Guinness pie. Just the sort of thing to stick to the ribs.

I opt for the steak and Guinness pie. Cooked in a small ceramic bowl, the pie features large chunks of stewing beef and chewy button mushrooms lathered in thick, savoury gravy and topped with a fine, flaky pastry crust. The meal is accompanied by baked potatoes and a squash and carrot mash. It goes so well with my pint of Brakspear bitter that I order another round and toast the general well-being of the realm.

During my travels, I have seen very little damage caused by the flood, and I am beginning to wonder about Richard's powers of observation. As I am exiting the Baskerville Arms, however, I bump into James, a neighbour who has just moved into Henley the previous week. He is the former dean of a major college in London, recently retired, and has the looks and air of an English academic, his pale blue eyes eternally staring over the bridge of his large thin nose at a point in the far distance. I ask if he has dropped in to Shiplake for a pint.

James pulls the stem of his pipe from his lips and points in the general direction of the river. "Unfortunately, I have other business. Come with me, and I'll show you."

We head down Bolney Road, a narrow, residential street that parallels the bank of the Thames. The asphalt is covered by a thick layer of mud. I follow James as best as I can, his long, thin legs striding over the branches and debris that litter the road. I finally catch up when he stops in front of his home, a renovated boathouse that was so badly damaged by New Year's floods that he and his wife were forced to temporarily move into Henley.

A small ceramic sign posted above the garage door announces the name of the abode: "House by the Water."

"At the height of the flood, you couldn't even get a car this far," says James. "We had to evacuate by canoe."

A blue dumpster parked by the road is loaded with scraps of carpet, a dishwasher, and furniture, all bearing the grime of water damage. The lot is narrow, barely eight metres wide, and the home located at the end is more than a hundred years old. "It was built by the Vicar of Kensington in 1902," notes James. We walk down a path through the garden to the house.

Outside, there is little evidence of damage. Except for some pods of drying mud in the garden, the grounds look relatively untouched—no worse than the after-effects of a storm, perhaps.

Inside is a different cauldron of carp, however. On the main floor, the bottom of an upright piano is covered with mud. Likewise, the wall plaster is rippled, and an ugly brown stain extends several feet up the walls. Commercial dehumidifiers are humming industriously away, but they cannot mask the musty smell of damp that now permeates the home.

"We had a party on December 28, and we noticed the river beginning to rise then," explains James. By New Year's Eve, when the river had begun to crest, it was still short of entering the main floor of their home, however, and they thought they would ride out the flood intact.

That was, until the Thames Authority decided to close the Thames Barrier. Built to protect London from flooding from the

North Sea, officials were forced to close the barrier at 9 PM on New Year's Day due to high tides. It acted like a stopper, slowing the flow of the river and backing it up.

"It rose so quickly that by morning there was two feet of water in the kitchen," says James. "Our neighbours came and helped us move books and family photos to the second floor, then we had to evacuate." By the time the water receded, almost £50,000 of damage had been done. James glances around at the sodden mess. "I guess we were fortunate."

It figures: I spend the day wandering about in the cold, wet rain, and Linda comes down with a bad chest cold. Fortunately, administering to the ill is one of the things I feel I do better than any other living person. I tuck her in under her duvet with a pile of magazines and several boxes of Kleenex, then tirelessly run up and down the stairs with steaming cups of mint tea, homemade chicken soup, and the occasional hot toddy to clear the sinuses. Someday, when I have gone to my just reward, they shall erect a bronze statue in my memory (nothing too ostentatious, please), and mothers will bring their children to admire it.

I am thinking of all this as I stand in line at the pharmacy clutching a drippy umbrella in one hand and a list of nostrums in the other. I love umbrellas. In fact, everyone in Britain loves umbrellas. An umbrella here is as indispensable as Prozac in a loony bin; you need to have it handy at all times to keep from going insane. Whenever it rains, portable displays of umbrellas sprout like spiny steel flowers on every street corner. I have yet to purchase an umbrella for the simple reason that, during the first few weeks of rain, I noticed that every shop had a convenient bucket full of used umbrellas standing by the front door. I helped myself to at least a half-dozen before realizing that the bucket was merely a spot to place your wet umbrella upon entering. (For what it was worth, I later returned the one that had two ribs poking out.)

Unfortunately, all of the remaining umbrellas in my collection are of the collapsible kind, which are excellent for tucking away in a knapsack but perfectly useless for goosing the woman standing at the counter in front of me. She is nattering away to the cashier about how expensive everything is these days, all the while scrounging around in a little leather purse for the exact change necessary to purchase a tube of denture adhesive. She finally manages to find the required pence among all the mothballs and mints lurking in her purse and shuffles off ...

"Sir?"

... In the direction of what I fervently hope is a careening bus ...

"Sir?"

... As I stare with envy at a man in the shaving cream aisle carrying an immense golf umbrella, and I fantasize about all that can be done with six inches of shiny metal tip ...

"*SIR?*"

I turn back to the pharmacist, whose face has gone a remarkable shade of red. It seems it's my turn. I place the box of Kleenex down on the counter. "I'd also like a bottle of nasal decongestant and a large pack of Tylenol."

"We only have pain relievers in packages of twelve."

"Then give me three packages."

"I'm sorry sir, but we're not allowed to sell more than one package at a time to customers."

Have you ever had that feeling where you just know the next question you ask is going to get a really stupid answer, yet you ask it anyway? "Why not?"

"It's to protect people from taking too many and committing suicide, sir."

"Fine. Sell me one pack and I'll go to the end of the line and come around again so you can sell me some more."

"We're not allowed to sell you more than one box a day."

I don't know whether to laugh or weep. I would have chosen the former, but I doubt they would have sold me more than one box of Kleenex, either. Bloody nanny state.

Linda finally recovers from her cold and, at the end of January, announces that she is ready to return to work. It is 7 AM, and I am looking out our bedroom window onto the river. The sun hasn't risen, but it's still light enough to see a mist descending from the low clouds. Only it isn't a mist, it is a million flakes, all huge, all falling with dreamlike abandon toward the earth. It looks like Owen won't have to take his kids to Lapland, after all.

By the time I set out to drive Linda to work, three inches of snow cover the car. I worry about the condition of the roads; will they ice up underneath the white layer? I eye my radials dubiously—they are designed for racing along dry roads at 190 kilometres per hour, not slogging through icy sludge. I decide to increase traction by loading up the trunk. Luckily, I just happen to have a large box of rejected manuscripts residing in the garage; finally, I have a good use for them.

Traffic is light through Henley, but the road up White Hill has turned into a toboggan run. Several sedans and light trucks have spun into the ditch. Traffic slows to a crawl and by the time we hit Wargrave Road, it is almost 8 AM.

For some reason or other, it is mandatory for school runs to be made by Range Rovers. Not Land Rovers, which have upholstery moulded from scrap steel and can go through two metres of mud, but the bloated road scows favoured by people who value a car by its number of cup holders. The mothers behind the wheel are clearly terrified, and respond by driving fifteen kilometres per hour lest their forty-five-centimetre knobby tires lose traction and slide out of control into the car in front, inflating air bags and damaging precious Harley Street nose jobs. It only takes two hours longer than normal to drop Linda off at work.

By the time I return to Henley, the sun is out and the land-scape is a brilliant, blinding white. I grab my camera and head south along the river towpath. A retired farmer, clad in flat cap and wellies, is taking his morning constitutional. His face is red and raw, and this is before he reaches the Anchor pub. I suspect he'll be the shade of a stoplight by the time he gets home tonight. The swans float along the side of the river, puzzled and suspicious of the fluffy white stuff clinging to the shore. They paddle over when I appear to take their picture, but are too wary to come close enough to beg for bread-crumbs.

My first stop is Marsh Lock, where the thin blanket of snow has dusted the lawns of the mansions overlooking the works. I take several pictures of towering evergreens, their verdant branches frosted with patches of white, thrilled at the opportunity to record something I've seen approximately eleven thousand times before in Canada. Pathetic, really, but it's one of those digital cameras with no film, so I can take all the pix I want and erase them from my computer later. I'm the disposable Ansel Adams.

When I get back to town, most of the snow on the streets has devolved into grey slush, obviating the need for anything as drastic as sweeping it off the sidewalk. I drop into the newsagent's, where Vinodhan is warily staring out the window. It turns out that he has never seen snow and, quite frankly, never wants to. In spite of my entreaties, he refuses to even go outside until the last of it has disappeared. He's managed to live all his life without the stuff, why risk pneumonia now? The rest of the town seems to have a similar attitude. A white-haired woman peers out of her bay window with a grim expression, no doubt assuming it to be some precursor to the four horsemen of the apocalypse. A postman huffs as he pushes his bright orange mail cart through the slush.

Fortunately, there are still a few residents left who retain the innate ability to relish the situation. A gang of boys aged eight or nine go running up Queen Street, armed with a selection of rotten fruit gleaned from the bin behind the greengrocer's. Suddenly, one of them spots a blanket of snow on a very new, very expensive Mercedes sports coupe parked in a handicapped space. Placing his runny Granny Smith upon the hood of the car, he reverentially gathers up a handful of the white stuff, expertly compacts it into a ball, and launches it at his comrades. Within seconds, the Mercedes is scraped clean of snow, its white, icy shawl replaced by a gift basket of mouldy bananas, pears, and apples.

I just love kids.

7

FEBRUARY

Cabin Fever

It is a filthy, rotten morning, even by British standards. Grey clouds, thick and low, loiter in the sky. The chestnut trees on the far hill are stripped bare, their skeletons black and gaunt. The river flows past, cold as steel. Everything is dark, dreary, and damp, an eon away from the distant memory of summer light that gives warmth and succour to the dark recesses of the soul.

Linda catches me writing this tripe in my diary as she prepares to leave for work. "What's wrong?"

"I can't stand this bloody weather."

"I can't either; let's go on a holiday somewhere warm. How about Spain?"

The thought cheers me up to no end, and I spend the morning making arrangements. Wary of our experience in the Canary Islands, I search the Internet for a destination unspoiled by British tourists. A website for the town of Marbella features a series of photographs of a languid Iberian town. The accompanying text assures me that it has retained the charm of the Old World, while offering the comforts of modern amenities at reasonable rates. What could be better than that? I book our flight and reserve a room in a resort on the edge of town.

By the time I have finished, it is almost noon. The weather is still grim; I decide that the only antidote is to cook for lunch that epitome of British cuisine, the jacket potato. I turn the oven on to warm it up then discover that the larder is bare of tubers. I reluctantly wrap a black wool scarf three times around my neck and head out the door.

When I arrive at Waitrose, I immediately head for the potato display in the grocery section. After closely examining the sultry red skin of the Desirees, I opt for the Maris Piper, its skin scrubbed to a soft, buttery gleam.

Now for the filling. There are some who admire the way that a topping of pork and beans cooked in tomato sauce harkens them back to their days at Harrow, but for them I recommend a caning on the backside. Others opt for more exotic thrills, such as the chicken marsala available at the deli counter, but for the true traditional recipe I always choose tuna. Not the fresh, glistening stuff available at the fish counter, of course, but the brine-soaked morsels packed in a tin. I always buy the brand that states that the enclosed tuna has been treated in a humane and conscientious manner, although I'm not quite sure what that entails. Perhaps it was allowed to write one last letter back home before having the flesh boiled from its bones.

I am ruminating so intently over the fine print that I fail to notice Alan until he runs over my foot with his shopping cart. "Awright?" he asks, leaving me to wonder if he is concerned over my bruised toe or merely offering the local salutation. I explain that I am planning to bake jacket potatoes for lunch. "That sounds brilliant! I love jacket potatoes!" I invite Alan to join me. "I'd love to," he replies and offers to give me a lift home. We make our purchases and go out to the parking lot. I follow as Alan heads toward a tiny blue automobile. It is a sports car, complete with fins, ram-charger scoops, and around five hundred barely contained horses.

"My God, what's that?"

"A Lotus," Alan says. "Hop in."

I am hesitant; not only does the car have a sinister look to it just standing still, but I clearly recall our wild drive through the countryside on our way to the Crooked Billet. I finally acquiesce to Alan's cheerful insistence, however, and reluctantly clamber in.

Alan shows me how to buckle the racing harness before stomping down on the gas pedal. We zoom back toward Boathouse Reach at a pace usually reserved for attempts to break the sound barrier.

"I had a bit of a scare recently," Alan shouts as he swerves around a baby carriage. "The doctor found this lump in my neck."

"Was it cancer?"

"Oh, no. It was from when I crashed my race car into a wall at 100 mph." Alan pulls into the parking lot and comes screeching to a halt in front of the house. I unbuckle my harness, grateful to be alive, and crawl out.

By this time the oven has reached sufficient temperature to warm up the entire kitchen. I give the spuds a good scrub and place them inside. Although some potatoes are ready within the hour, I prefer to allow them ninety minutes in order for the complex carbohydrates to break down into sweeter sugars. In the meantime, I open the tuna can, drain the brine, and prepare the filling. The most important ingredient is, of course, mayonnaise. While there are some purists who insist upon whipping it up fresh themselves, I find that sort of obsession bordering on, well, *French*, and opt for the bottled version. A dash of salt and pepper, a spoon of minced green onion, a healthy dose of fresh dill, and a squeeze of lemon complete the recipe.

While the potatoes are cooking, Alan and I go upstairs to watch a rugby game. Back in the Middle Ages, the French celebrated the beginning of Lent in February with a game called a mêlée. Supposedly, it was invented to celebrate the expulsion of the Vikings and the invention of beer. At any rate, two gangs of young louts from adjacent villages would try to advance an inflated pig bladder through the use of kicking, kidney punches, and flying fists against their opponents. Feasts of pancakes and much drinking followed the contests, and then a riot. Not surprisingly, the mêlée was greatly popular in England. Apparently, King Richard II banned the game in the fourteenth century because it interfered with archery practice and general health. There was no point in wasting money on defence, he reasoned, if a football game will do a better job of decimating the troops than the opposing army.

Once the potato has been rescued from the oven and its steaming innards exposed, a light coating of butter is *de rigueur*. After the filling has been heaped in, some gourmets add a topping of chopped fresh coriander or parsley. We take our plates into the dining room, where I devour every succulent morsel, including the papery skin. The warm, creamy meal penetrates to every corner of my inner being. Outside the patio doors, the cruel wind howls and the trees rattle, but inside it is toasty, warm, and safe.

"Beastly weather," says Alan.

"We're going to take a week and go to Marbella."

Alan looks up from his lunch. "Do you want me to water your plants while you're gone?"

It's such a simple question, really, yet I am taken aback. Frankly, I never expected anyone in Henley to acknowledge our presence beyond mere politeness, let alone volunteer help. That isn't to say that the people of Henley aren't generous, it's just, well, I didn't think this sort of thing was *done* here.

There is something refreshingly egocentric about Henley-on-Thames. It is all about *itself*, not somebody else's conception. That's not to say that Henley is alone in this aspect. One only has to go to the Cotswolds to find it in spades. We once attended a wedding near Stow-on-the-Wold and were put up in the home of friends of the bride's. Tony and Mary had a wonderful cottage of buttery sandstone nestled into a tiny, picture postcard–perfect village just off the main highway. Their town hadn't suffered privations from tourists primarily because the streets were too narrow for buses, but, nonetheless, they feared it was only a matter of time before their village became commercialized.

"Why don't you simply change the name to Sodoff?" I offered. "That way, whenever a stranger stopped to ask you where they were, you could simply say, 'Sod off!'" Our hosts thought this an eminently workable idea, but I don't know if it was ever adopted, as I backed my car over their hedge in a mildly inebriated state and they never responded to the Christmas card we sent.

At any rate, Henley doesn't need to change its name; it has an air that no road sign could ever equal. It sits in the valley, self-luminous, sure of itself. When you enter the town limits, you are in the-one-and-only-Henley, and you can take it as is, or you can turn right around and leave, thank you very much. Frankly, I find this attitude immensely refreshing.

So that is why I am so astounded, nay, *shocked*, by the offer, because it's not just an invitation to do some household chore; no, it's much more—it's the moment when you suddenly *belong*. When your neighbours stop looking *at* you, and start looking *after* you. I pride myself on being a good neighbour. It's true, I gossip and pry and spend far too much time minding other people's business, but that, in my opinion, is simply indicative of someone who cares. For those who have lived in one place all their lives, neighbourliness is a given, like the sun coming up in the morning, but if you have resided all over the world, as I have, then you know that it takes time and effort and not a little luck to become a true neighbour.

In Paris, it took a year for many of our Gallic neighbours to break through their traditional reserve and become sufficiently intrigued about our presence to root through our garbage. But here it is, barely five months into our sojourn in Henley, and already someone has extended a warm hand in greeting. I take out my key ring and remove the front-door key and hand it to Alan. "I'd be delighted. By the way, help yourself to anything you want."

"Brilliant." Alan finishes his potato. "I hope you don't mind if your lingerie gets stretched a bit."

According to Richard, my article will appear in the *Standard* this Friday. On the appointed day, I scurry down to the newsagent's. My photograph is just above "Thought for the Week," the vicar's regular column. I am wearing my Canada T-shirt and grinning like a drunk caught pissing on the church wall. Does it get any better than this?

I take two copies up to Vinodhan, who regards my purchase with mild confusion. "Why are you buying two *Standard*s?"

"Because my picture is in this week's issue. See?"

Vinodhan stares at it closely. "That is not you—this man is too handsome."

"Thanks." I take all the compliments I can get, even the back-handed ones.

I decide my best course of action would be to head down-town, where my adoring public has a better chance of spontane-ously bumping into me. I proceed to wander through the town square, amiably nodding to people I don't know and generally trying to show my best profile, to no avail. I stop to buy some tulips from Jackie the flower girl, but if she's seen my mug in the paper, she hides it well. Even a tour of Waitrose, with the paper prominently tucked under my arm, doesn't do the trick. Man, this is one tough town.

I am returning down Reading Road when the skies open up. Like a fool, I have walked out the door without an umbrella. I dive into Chateau du Vin and join Richard. Behind the bar, Ricardo is holding the phone a good foot away from his ear as a torrent of passionate Portuguese loudly spills out of the earpiece.

"But Bébé, I love you!" he shouts over the barrage. The reply is an audible click at the other end of the line, then silence. Ricardo hangs up the phone and turns his attention back to us, a hangdog expression on his face.

"Everything all right?" I ask.

"It is my fiancée."

"She misses you?"

"No." Ricardo shrugs a *what-can-you-do?* "She found out about my girlfriend."

Before I can offer any words of consolation, Felix appears from the kitchen. "*Ça va!* You come Valentine's Day, no? Very special menu!" He kisses the tips of his fingers. "*Magnifique!*"

I am about to make a reservation for a table for two, but then, when I see what the *prix fix* is for the evening, I have second thoughts. "Richard, I forgot to ask—what do you pay for an article in the *Standard*?"

"Eighteen pence a line."

Not exactly going to cover the *hors d'oeuvres*, then. Somewhat deflated, I return home, where Owen is having a smoke outside his office door. "*Oy!*" he shouts. "There was a big black limo with a Canadian flag just here looking for you!"

I crane my neck back and forth, peering up the street. "Did they say what they wanted?"

"Your passport. They said you was a turncoat."

Bless him. At least one person in this town cares enough to take the piss.

When I arrive at the door, I find a flyer tucked in the front mail slot. The Tiger Lily Lady's Shoppe, on Duke Street, is having a special late-night shopping event for men. The flyer promises the following:

"Free glass of wine or beer. Free gift wrapping service. And, may we remind you gentlemen to check your Valentine's sizes as 'this big' is not good enough!"

What an excellent idea for Linda's present. Unfortunately, the flyer lists some suggested lingerie ensembles on the back, with prices that should include a lingerie model. I sigh. It is time for me to take a desperate move; I must find work.

Up to this point, one might conclude that my value extends no further than baked potatoes, but I do have a few marketable skills. For the last quarter century or so I have been delighting magazine readers with scintillating tales of how to live in a teepee and the correct way to varnish player pianos. It's more of a gift, really. At any rate, I have a few freelance opportunities to explore in London, and the next morning, I board the *Henley Bullet*.

The train trundles slowly through the countryside, past horse paddocks and fields covered with winter stubble, until it reaches the rail bridge that crosses over the river. Geologists say the Thames has been here for quite less time than you might imagine; for hundreds of thousands of years it flowed to the northeast, on the vast plain that stretches through Oxfordshire and the fens out onto the Wash. But the Ice Age came along and it was routed through a gap in the Chilterns near Goring, and it has only been for the last twelve thousand years or so that it has followed its current course.

In fact, it's been much shorter than that. For a river knows no bounds, only the dictates of gravity. It will, over time, cut through the strongest rock, carving its way laterally with inexorable force. Then it will suddenly stop and choose an entirely new course, one that takes it far afield. If you were to pick a spot in the Thames Valley, even one several miles from the river's current location, and dig down, you would come across the telltale fluvial sand and boulders, relict evidence that the Thames once coursed through this arid spot, strong and clear and untamed. Of course, that no longer holds true. The river is a prisoner, caged by the steel that encloses its banks, forced into a path of man's making. But not forever. Some day another glacier will come along and scrape up the town hall and St. Mary's Church and all the rest and dump it all into the English Channel.

On the plus side, it would also get rid of Twyford Station. Designed by bureaucrats with Seeing Eye dogs, it is an eyesore of epic proportions, a crusty concoction of brick, concrete, and rusty steel girders. I disembark and stand at the edge of the platform; mercifully, the connecting train to Paddington Station arrives within a few minutes. It is mid-morning, and the carriage is half empty; a businessman takes a chair directly opposite me. He is in his late fifties, with an expanse of bald skull, a dark grey suit, and a blue silk tie spotted with tiny gold crests. He places a cup of coffee down upon the tiny window ledge and opens his *Times*, only to be interrupted by the ringing of his cellphone.

Now, I am not one of those people who automatically cringe when someone pulls out their cell in a confined space and entertains everyone with a ninety-decibel recitation of their recent bowel surgery; in fact, I rather enjoy the opportunity to update my hypochondria. What I do object to, however, is the waft of breath that emanates from his mouth. It is so bad that even my ears wince. It is, as far as my abused nostrils can ascertain, a mix of last Sunday's pork roast still lingering between his bicuspids and the cherry mocha coffee that is currently swishing past his tonsils. I politely ask if he would object if I open the overhead window to let in a draft of air. As it turns out, we are just passing the Slough sewage works, but the aroma that blows in is still a blessed relief from the alternative.

The train eventually arrives in Paddington Station, and, in accordance with the government's mandate that everyone get more exercise, we disembark on a platform about a kilometre and a half west of the main terminal. I hike to the tube station entrance and descend into the bowels of the earth until I come to the Bakerloo line. There is something about the London Underground that immediately induces crankiness in me; as soon as a train full of sweaty commuters pulls into the station, my inner Scrooge emerges. If Julie Andrews herself were to come flouncing down the escalator in a pinafore trilling away about the fresh Tyrolean air, I swear I'd hoist her onto the track.

Fortunately, the car is half empty, and I find an empty seat, one that offers a first-rate view of the advertising billboards posted above everyone's head. One, in particular, catches my attention. *Care for a Dip?* It appears there is a new attraction in town called the Wetland Centre where, according to the accompanying photograph, you can dangle your squirmy child above a variety of carnivorous reptile ponds. Upon reading the fine print, I discover that it is some sort of science park for junior Darwins. Talk about missing an opportunity.

I exit the Oxford Street tube station and head for my friend's office. Chris is the editor of a petroleum magazine; for the last several years, he has been assigning me work on such fascinating subjects as oil pipelines and what to do about excess gas. He is partial to obscure statistics and prone to losing his glasses on his head. Not only does he always have the most unusual stories to recount, but he is most attentive to buying rounds while doing so.

We meet in his favourite business venue, the Windsor Arms pub. It is my turn to buy the rounds, so after ordering a pint of bitter for myself and a gin and tonic for Chris, we settle into a corner booth.

"I must tell you what happened to me last month," he starts. "I was having these dizzy spells. I thought it was just an inner-ear infection, but my wife Jane insisted I go see a doctor."

Naturally, the doctor suspected a brain tumour. She referred Chris to a clinic, where they ordered him to remove all items of metal from his person before strapping him down to a gurney and rolling him into the middle of an MRI scanner. Chris tried to warn them that he had some staples in his head from a childhood accident, but they wouldn't listen. The technicians fired up the hundred-thousand-volt magnet and it promptly shot sparks in sundry directions. They quickly stopped the device and extracted Chris before he started attracting key rings. A week later, when he went back to the doctor to get the news on the test, she had absolutely no idea who he was. The doctor mined through her in-tray in a fruitless search for his file, pausing to read a few Christmas cards and other items of interest, until she finally gave up searching.

"Have you had any recurrence of the dizzy spells?" she asked.

"No," said Chris.

"In that case, it was probably just an inner-ear infection."

Chris downs his G&T in one gulp. "And she wonders why my blood pressure is so high." He hands his empty glass to me. "I do believe that calls for another round."

In fact, it calls for several rounds, during which Chris assigns me a lucrative series of stories to write. When I finally stagger out to the tube and head back to Paddington Station, I barely make it in time to catch the five o'clock train back to Twyford. Of course, there is no room to sit down, which I don't really mind, as I have an overwhelming urge to use the loo anyway.

There is an ongoing debate in the national press about the deplorable state of education in Britain, especially the piffling amount that kids learn about their own country. In my opinion, the UK's vast educational resources would best be directed toward teaching people how to pee in a moving train.

The water closet is liberally sprinkled with urine, the result of male persons not knowing how to properly empty their bladders at eight kilometres per hour. I suspect that it requires a lateral movement timed to coincide with the lurching of the train as it rides over the decrepit tracks, but since I haven't the foggiest idea how to do it, either, by the time I am finished, I am heartily wishing I had worn my wellies.

When I arrive home, Linda greets me at the door. "The fan in the bathroom is making that funny sound again."

Rather than lying down for a snooze, I ill-advisedly go upstairs and inspect the culprit. The fan has been wired to the light switch so as to turn on whenever the room is illuminated, on the not-unreasonable assumption that it will need airing out at some point in the proceedings. The problem is that this particular fixture has developed a noise like a swarm of bees in a cardboard box. Not only that, but a built-in timer means that the noise continues for twenty minutes after the light is switched off.

I drag a portable ladder from the garage and clamber up to inspect the fan. Removing the cover, I discover several generations' worth of detritus built up around the electric motor. There is enough fluff, lint, dead skin, and other ossified effluvia to knit a poncho. I remove the intimate remains of several previous tenants and place it in the closest thing I have to a biohazard receptacle, a Tesco bag. I finish reinstalling the fan cover and take a step back to admire my work. The only problem is, I have forgotten I am standing on a ladder. I tumble backward and crack the back of my skull smartly on the doorknob.

Linda comes rushing up from the living room. "What happened?"

Dazed, I point to the offending doorknob. "I fell and hit my head."

Linda examines the knob. "There doesn't seem to be any damage."

"What about *me*?" Linda sighs patiently as she presses a cloth over my wound and we head downtown toward the Henley Surgery.

I don't know what is worse, the pain or the thought of going to the NHS. I have visions of becoming a human magnet. When we reach the Henley Surgery, the receptionist takes one look and offers a snap prognosis. "Bumped our head, did we?"

"No, I like to style my hair with ketchup. Is there a doctor who can see me?"

"Certainly." She takes out a clipboard. "If you could just answer a few questions. Are you on medication?"

"No."

"Does anyone in your family suffer from epilepsy?"

"No."

"Do you have any sexually transmitted diseases?"

"Why, are you asking me out on a date?"

Linda orders me to sit in the waiting room while she completes the forms. Honestly, where do they hire such nincompoops? I feel a little dizzy, but I vow to stay awake, certain that if I pass out, I shall wake up with my feet sewn back on the wrong legs.

I am shown into an examination room, and a doctor soon appears. She is tall and thin, with greying hair. "Let's have a look, shall we?" She turns my head and examines the wound briefly. "Any dizziness?"

"A bit."

"*Hmmn*." Uh-oh, here comes the CAT scan. Instead, she takes out a penlight and examines my eyes, then peers into my ears. "Fortunately, your skull is quite thick. Everything looks all right." She swabs my neck and places a plaster on the wound. "Contact me if you start feeling faint. Otherwise, you should be fine."

And that was that. No muss, no fuss, no pus. Really, Chris is such a wimp.

Valentine's Day arrives, and, newly energized with funds, I head down to Market Place to buy my sweetheart some gifts. My first stop is the flower stall, where I pick out a dozen red roses. It is a frosty, grey morning, and the girls have been fortifying their immune system with gin from their coffee Thermos. "*Ooh*, someone's gonna get lucky tonight when she sees these," cackles Pauline as she leans over to goose me. I beat a hasty retreat before they decide to offer some personal tips.

Fortunately, the staff at Waitrose is more sedate, and I am not molested as I gather some champagne and a few appetizers into my red plastic shopping basket and head for the checkout counter. Mabel, a large, dark-haired clerk with the incisors of a chipmunk, is wearing a hair clip that sports two red hearts bobbing on steel springs in honour of the day. She stops in mid-swipe as she is ringing my purchases through.

"*Ooh*," she announces, pointing to a dark green spot on the cheddar. "You got some mouldy cheese here, Love. You know, me dear husband always used to eat mouldy cheese—he loved it. Mind, he died at the age of fifty-two."

"Sorry to hear that," I say. "Food poisoning?"

"No, he got hit by a bus." She puts the cheese under the counter and nods to me wisely. "Just goes to show, you can't be too careful." Or too sane, apparently.

On the way back, I stop by Chateau du Vin. Claude is behind the bar, doing double duty as bartender and lunchtime waiter.

"Where's Ricardo today?"

"Disappeared," says Claude over his shoulder.

"Did a runner back to his gal in Portugal," says Teddy, who is having his lunch at the counter. He nods toward the till, "From what I hear, there's a few things missing, as well."

Ah, the heartbreak of romance. Without a doubt, Henley's most tragic case of love gone wrong is that of Mary Blandy, the fetching daughter of Francis Blandy, a lawyer and Henley's town clerk. In 1751, she fell in love with Captain Cranstoun, renowned for his ugly appearance and married status. When the father naturally opposed the affair, Cranstoun sent Mary a magic potion purchased from a Scottish witch with the instructions to mix it in her father's food. He promptly fell seriously ill and died. Mary tried to flee, but only made it as far as the Little Angel pub on the Buckinghamshire side of the river, where a mob cornered her. She was arrested and executed in Oxford in April 1752. In thanks for their contribution to her demise, she returned to haunt various locales on special occasions, including Valentine's Day.

It is the prospect of sighting Mary that inspires Richard and me to visit the Little Angel that afternoon. The pub is divided into two sections, the original, low-ceilinged cottage dating back some four hundred years, and a new, octagonal conservatory large enough to hold ten tables. The latter is rather swank, more suitable for an anniversary celebration than an apparition, so we have stationed ourselves in the old pub, where one is generally encouraged to drink beer while watching for spectral emanations.

"You really believe in ghosts?" asks Richard over our pints of Brakspear.

"Absolutely. I once saw a ghost in the men's room in the Gold Dust Saloon in San Francisco."

"Really! How did you know it was a ghost?"

"He was headless."

Richard nods thoughtfully. "That's generally a sure sign. How many pints did you have before seeing the ghost?"

"Nine, but it was American beer."

Richard and I buy several more rounds in the name of paranormal investigation. We survey the pub, but in spite of our diligence, Mary refuses to appear. "Well, that's enough for tonight," announces Richard. "I must get home to greet Jan."

"Got anything special planned for Valentine's?"

"Four hours of love-making."

"That's impressive."

"Not really. Three hours and fifty-five minutes of that is begging."

I get home in time to serve champagne and nibblies to Linda, then it is off to Chateau du Vin. In place of Ricardo, Claude has rounded up Miguel, a temporary waiter from Spain. He escorts us to our table and asks our pleasure. We order a rosé champagne from the cave of Michel Gonet, in Epernay. Miguel makes a great flourish of removing the cork, managing to keep most of wine in the bottle.

Felix rushes out to give Linda two scratchy kisses. "*Ça-va?*" he bellows, and I catch the hint of more than just a little cooking wine on his breath. "I have something very special for you!" As hoped, Felix has ordered in a large quantity of *foie gras*. In anticipation, we have brought our own bottle of Chateau de Monbazillac, which Miguel obligingly opens. Felix soon returns with two plates laden with slices of goose liver lightly fried in butter, served on a bed of cooked figs, and covered in a sublime reduction of wine and Grand Marnier.

We barely have time for the appetizer to settle before Felix reappears with the main course, lamb chops grilled in garlic and olive oil, served with a delightful assortment of freshly steamed vegetables and roasted potatoes.

By now, the restaurant has filled up and Claude is helping Miguel behind the bar. Specifically, he is helping himself to several glasses of wine, and is soon in such a convivial mood that he un-characteristically begins to offer patrons free samples of whatever he happens to be holding. We are treated to several rather delight-ful glasses of white Graves, until, much to Claude's astonishment, the bottle runs dry.

Just as Claude wanders off to find a replacement, Felix reap-pears with our dessert, a sublime *crème brulée* lightly spiced with fresh vanilla. As we sit finishing our Monbazillac, I have the op-portunity to observe how well Latin blood responds to Valentine's Day. Miguel, his hair oiled into tight curls, is flirting shamelessly with every woman in the bar. I suspect he will either go home with someone else's wife or be run over by a Bentley. Most likely both. We pay the bill then stop at the kitchen door on the way out to thank Felix. Once again, he is dancing in his flip-flops with the sous chef and swigging from a champagne bottle. We wave *adieu*, and step into the night.

I have barely recovered from Valentine's Day by the time we leave the following week for Marbella. After the cold and rain of England, the hot, dry weather of Costa del Sol is like heaven. The sky is a beautiful clear blue, and the Mediterranean winks at us in the distance. We wander across the main road from the airport, pick up our rental car, and head off for the resort.

The philosophy of the average Spanish driver is somewhat different than that encountered in Canada; as close as I can tell, it is a mix of Catholic faith and kamikaze fatalism. Within the first kilometre, I realize that I must either adapt or die. Reaching down beneath the wheel, I rip the brake pedal off its mount and fling it out the window. I snap off the turn signal and toss it onto the highway, as well. Amazingly, I am suddenly filled with a liberating rush of joy that transcends all borders. Hammering down on the gas, I surge ahead, flitting between propane tankers and dynamite lorries, secure in the knowledge that Jesus is watching over me. Ah, welcome to Spain.

In contrast to the highway, the Don Carlos Hotel is an oasis of calm, with more than four hectares of gardens. After checking into the hotel, we wander down to the Olympic-sized sundeck. The entire complex is about sixty metres long and sixty metres wide, with three levels. The upper level is an outdoor extension of the main restaurant, with a large pool surrounded by a phalanx of blue-and-white-tiled Corinthian columns. The bottom level has a kidney-shaped wading pool, ideal for banishing noisy children, while the main section has a large swimming pool and hundreds of deck chairs.

It is here that we plop down to enjoy a few hours of relaxation. The surrounding pine trees frame a brilliant blue sky, and the sound of cicadas fills the air. The smell of the ocean, a mix of salty sea and the distant Sahara, is marred only by the odour of Pine Sol and lard emanating from the suntan lotion on the fat Englishman sitting upwind of us. I use the term Englishman only as a vague approximation; he has a cellphone clamped permanently to his ear, and whenever he opens his mouth, which is a lot, the sound that emanates from it contains absolutely no consonants, or, for that matter, English. As a result, a short exclamatory sentence, such as, "I would like to get myself one of those," comes out something like "*Oy ga uh ge me wuh a ose.*" His wife has the look of someone who wishes her husband would take a separate holiday, perhaps to visit his relatives at the La Brea Tar Pits. We decide to abandon the pool and go investigate Marbella.

Old Marbella turns out to be a treat. Much to Linda's delight, the tiny shops along the narrow, cobbled lanes seem to be largely occupied by shoe stores, and it takes about three hours to walk the hundred metres to the centre of town.

The Plaza del los Naranjos, a pleasing square filled with orange trees, is lined with a series of restaurants and cafés. We choose a wonderful little *churreria*, a coffee shop that specializes in churros, or Spanish donuts. Ordering a hot chocolate, we rip off chunks of fried batter that has been twisted into a swirl, not unlike a long line of sausage. Dipping the end into the chocolate, we slurp down as much of the concoction that escapes our clothing. Later, wandering around the town, we find a delightful tapas bar, where we have a lunch of Spanish ham, toasted goat cheese, and pork in tomato sauce, all washed down with excellent, cold beer.

By the time it is siesta, we are more than ready to head back to the hotel, where, after a refreshing bottle of Cava, we go in search of dinner. We head down the beach and wander along the endless shore until we come to a restaurant on the edge of the sea. It's not much to look at—little more than a shack covered in palm leaves—but the smell of garlic frying in olive oil and the lively laughter emanating from the diners inside is more than enough to lure us in. We take a seat on the patio and order the house specialty: white fish baked in salt. We while away the half-hour it takes to prepare by sipping on an effervescent bottle of wine and watching the sunset.

The waitress finally arrives with a large platter of coarse salt, which she taps into chunks and lifts away to reveal a whole fish steaming delicately in the candlelight. She carefully debones the fish and serves the succulent meat, along with fresh, buttery beans, and roasted garlic potatoes.

We eat our meal and linger under the stars, with only one thought in my mind.

I wonder if Alan is really going to try on the lingerie?

8

MARCH

Spring Has Sprung

When we arrive back from our week in Spain, the ground around Henley is still damp, cold, and lifeless. The north wind howls down from the Chilterns, chilling the marrow, and rain pounds down almost incessantly. But crocuses, both yellow and purple, are poking their tiny heads out of the long expanse of grass in Mill Meadows.

Well then. It must be spring.

The advent of spring, of course, means that it is time for all Brits to migrate outdoors. It doesn't matter if the wind is blowing sleet sideways; the appearance of crocuses, which will erupt through fifteen centimetres of snow, means it's time to put out the patio furniture and get some fresh air.

Richard has invited me to lunch. The temperature is slightly above the point where starlings freeze in mid-air, and ugly grey clouds are scudding dangerously low over the adjacent buildings, but Claude has opened up the garden behind Chateau du Vin, so we are having our meal outside.

"Garden" is a rather fulsome description of the tiny space—a garbage bin with rhododendron beds and lawn furniture is a more accurate depiction. I arrive and am escorted out back; Richard has already ordered our first course: soup, the better to hold down the *Times* and keep it from blowing away.

As I approach, he glances up briefly. "Did you see this article on George Harrison?" Richard is interested in all things

Harrison, not so much because he admires his music, but because the former Beatle lived in a huge estate on the western edge of Henley for more than thirty years, and like all good newspapermen, Richard has taken a proprietary interest in anyone unlucky enough to live within his purview. "Someone paid £1,000 for a lock of George's hair."

I chip through the skiff of ice forming on my tomato and basil soup. "Who'd be nuts enough to pay that?"

Planting both elbows firmly upon the page, Richard reads further. "Some barber from Barcelona, apparently. At least it beat out Michael Jackson's shoes. They only sold for eight hundred."

A few days ago, I had passed the gate to Harrison's estate, Friar Park, a frothy concoction of wrought iron and multicoloured brick. Unfortunately, the gate was closed and signs against trespassing had been posted warning away varmints, miscreants, and the morbidly curious, which more or less describes me. "You ever go up to Harrison's home?" I ask.

"No, his widow doesn't allow anyone in." Richard pulls out a pen and turns to the *Times* crossword puzzle. "I did interview the architect who did all the renovations, though."

My interest is suddenly piqued. "Think he'd talk to me?"

Richard, already lost in his puzzle, absently shrugs. "Why not? He's retired, but he still lives in town."

I thank Richard and, braced by lunch, I head back home along the river. In spite of the fact that the wind is churning the Thames into a froth, the marina crew is busy pulling motor launches from storage, spurred on no doubt by the imminent arrival of parka-clad tourists eager for an outing on an icebreaker. The main office for Andy's marina is a small brick cottage adjacent to the docks; smoke is rising from the chimney, and I decide to stop in and warm up.

There's something fine and masculine about a marina office. The thick pine floors have been roughened by a century of wear and tear. An ancient iron safe squats in one corner. The walls are decorated with aerial photos of Henley and the river, a rack of keys, and a broken chunk of oar. The aroma of pipe smoke and diesel hangs in the air.

Jack is at the main desk, working at his computer. Andy's eldest son is very keen about the Internet and is working on a new website for the marina. Andy is hovering nearby with the look of someone who would rather shave with sandpaper than touch a keyboard.

"Did you hear what happened the other morning?" he exclaims when I arrive. "Somebody stole Matthew Pinsent's new car from his house just up the road." Apparently, in the middle of the night, burglars approached the Olympic rowing champion's front door and stuck a magnet-tipped fishing pole through the letter flap and lifted the keys to his new Mercedes off a hallway counter.

"Fortunately, the car had a GPS tracker in it," interjects Jack. "The police located it the next day."

"*Humph*," replies Andy. "What's this world coming to?" He goes back to his corner office and sits down heavily in his chair in a manner that clearly defines his delight in all things modern. The office is definitely a little too warm for comfort and I make a hasty exit.

Outside, Edwina is leading Princess on her daily constitutional. "Foreigners," sniffs Edwina, when I repeat the tale of the stolen auto. "They steal a car and the next thing you know it's in Romania."

"Maybe it's locals. After all, lots of people around here own fishing poles."

Edwina shakes her head. "Not likely."

"Why? An Englishman's too honest?"

"Too lazy."

By this time, I've had enough fresh spring air to contract pneumonia, and head home for a nice cup of warm tea. I am hardly in the house, however, when the doorbell rings.

Owen is standing at the threshold, peering back over his shoulder. "*Oy*, do me a favour? I bought some tools off some blokes. Can I use your garage for a minute?"

"Sure." Owen eagerly scurries off, and I head back to the kitchen to plug in the kettle. I am interrupted, however, by a din in the garage. I go back out to discover a blue van has been backed up against the door and Owen and two strangers are busy unloading green plastic tool cases. I stare in disbelief as the pile approaches the roof. "What's all *this*?"

Owen opens one to reveal a cordless electric drill. "Nice, huh?"

In spite of Edwina's pronouncement about the local aversion to work, I can't help but think there's a certain amount of initiative going on here. In less time than it takes to strip the wheels off a Porsche, the men have finished unloading the goods.

"Well, I guess we'll be off to Cork then," says the short, fat one. They all shake hands and depart.

I shout after Owen. He turns, and I point to the pile of tools sitting in my garage in broad daylight. "Forget something?"

"Oh, right," Owen says. "Close the door, would you?"

I'm still staring numbly at the pile of tools when Owen returns a few minutes later and backs his estate wagon up to the door. "'Ere, give me a hand." I deem it wise to don a pair of work gloves before touching anything. "*Oy*, clever," says Owen. "Why didn't I think of that?"

As quickly as possible, we load everything into the boot. "This isn't what it looks like," says Owen. "Just a couple of lads with some excess stock they want to sell."

"At a five-finger discount, no doubt."

"More like ten."

At that moment, Kim the marine engineer walks around the corner. Owen throws a blanket over the boxes and then turns to me and places a finger over his lips. "*Shh.*" He pulls out a package of cigarettes and tries to nonchalantly light a fag.

Kim instantly spots the guilty look on Owen's face. "What you up to then?"

Owen coughs. "I bought some tools."

Kim glances in the back of the car. "What, fifty of 'em?"

"It isn't what it looks like."

Kim lifts the rear hatch, pulls back the blanket, and peers closely at the boxes. "These is nicked!"

"No, they ain't."

"Sure, there's some driver sitting up at the other end of the road in an empty lorry wondering what's happened to 'em."

"Jesus, keep it down, would you?" Owen tosses the cigarette to the ground and climbs into the driver's seat. As the car furtively sneaks off, Kim bursts into laughter.

I stare at the engineer. "What are you laughing at? He might get arrested for fencing stolen property."

"They ain't stolen. I was just taking the piss. Ol' Owen's been conned, he 'as."

"What do you mean?"

Kim tucks his hands into his coverall pockets and saunters off. "You just wait and see."

The change of weather over the next few days makes me forget about Owen and his tools. A warm southern wind blows up the valley, bringing with it the smell of young hay warming in the sun. Almost overnight, the tree that has been squatting like a spindly troll in one corner of our parking lot has burst into a mass of pink blossoms, and daffodils erupt in the roundabouts on the A4.

There is a sense of weight to the air, not just the fulsome tang of spring, but something headier. It's as though the flowers and trees are penetrating down through the ground and drawing up something more profound than mere nutrients; they are siphoning the very essence of the land itself, something that extends well beyond recorded history, back into something deeper, darker, primordial—the Stone Age.

Not a lot is known about the Stone Age in the UK—it's not like the Ink Age, which lends itself to posterity with much greater facility. This is a pity, because they seem to have been a lively bunch hereabouts. For instance, there is a long line of deep pits dug atop the Chilterns dating back some eight thousand years, just after the last continental glacier scooted back to Iceland. Nobody seems to have even the remotest idea of why they were built—were they fortifications or some form of celestial orientation in relation to ancient beliefs? Perhaps they were just big urinals. It's important not to overthink these things, you know.

At any rate, I drag my bicycle out of the garage, load up my backpack, and head out on a fact-finding expedition. My destination is the Highmoor Trench, which runs near the Ridgeway on the other side of the Chilterns. The Ridgeway itself may be one of the oldest highways in existence, dating back to 4000 B.C., when the Britons used a pathway starting at Overton Hill near Avebury and running some 137 kilometres in a northeast direction to Luton, where they could catch a low-cost flight to Ibiza. Circular forts, burial mounds, and settlements have been found all along the way, as well as more mysterious constructions, such as Grim's Ditch, a straight moat running five kilometres east of Wallingford, and the Highmoor Trench, which runs off at a tangent from the Ridgeway toward Henley.

I set off on my bike in a westerly direction. After pedalling through several featureless suburbs, I pick up a bridle path behind

Henley College. Almost immediately I find myself in the countryside. I ride along on a path edged on one side by a pasture and on the other by a row of willows that have been trimmed to create a long tunnel of overarching branches. The jarring sounds of town life recede and, except for the trilling of birds carried on the downslope wind, all is quiet.

I come to a gate in a wooden fence. Wherever public pathways cross fences, stiles are supplied to aid in clambering over the gates, which are invariably padlocked. Here, however, a woodpecker has chewed the end off the topmost beam, and a vandal, or perhaps a Viking, has severed the rest with a solid kick. I lift my bike over the remnants and continue on.

The Chiltern Hills rise some 152 metres above Henley. My plan is to make that climb as gradually as possible, and I follow a route that winds up a gently sloping valley. Pastureland spreads out on both sides of me, a herd of black-and-white cattle grazing far away on a hill. Something catches my eye in the pasture. About thirty metres away are two dead foxes, their carcasses picked by scavengers. A bird, possibly a red kite, lies nearby, its wings contorted in death. It is, no doubt, an unwitting victim of poison set out to control the fox population. But it does make a charming little Gothic touch to leaven an otherwise idyllic scene, that.

I work my way uphill, a layer of reddish mud making my wheels slip dangerously to the side. Now and again I stop to lift my bike over a fence, but other than dodging the occasional cow patty, the climb is one of those experiences that are good for you, and it fills me so full of vigour that, when I reach the top, I immediately lie down for a nap.

When I awake, I note that I am virtually at the doorstep of Grey's Court. I love old buildings with some history to them. The estate was built by Lord de Grey, who fought at the Battle of Crécy in France during the Hundred Years' War. Edward III was so enamoured of his valour that he gave the nobleman the right to crenellate.

And crenellate he did. The octagonal tower, pretty much all that remains of the original structure, is topped by a row of tooth-like masonry squares that allow archers to fire down upon unruly peasants with impunity, something that every lord cherishes. Unfortunately, the estate is closed, and I must comfort myself with the occasional peek over the high brick wall that rings the grounds.

When I stop for a moment's rest at the edge of the estate, a flock of chocolate-brown sheep come over to mooch. Unfortunately, I don't have so much as an apple on me, but I promise them I shall rectify the matter when I return later in the year to view the extensive gardens. The lad repairing a hole in the fence gives me a funny look. I get back on my bike and hastily continue my journey; perhaps I'd been talking to his girlfriend.

I pause near the top of the hill to get my bearings. According to the map, I'm close to the Highmoor Trench. Parking my bike against a tree, I set off into the forest in search of my quarry. At first, I am unsure if I'm heading in the right direction, but then I stumble across a discarded tube of caulking, surely evidence that I am close. And then I spot it—without a doubt, it is the most unimpressive engineering works I have seen in a long time. As a guess, I would say its ancient creators spent about one afternoon scraping back half a metre of muck in a straight line for about ninety metres. While archaeologists are puzzled about the function of these trenches, a modern-day government employee would recognize it immediately; it is a canal that was supervised by the public works department. These Stone Age people were a lot more advanced than we give them credit for.

I return to my bike and take a forest path that leads to another trench, this one in the Lambridge Wood. Now that I know what to expect, I quickly spot a shallow indentation running between a copse of beech trees. Something partially buried beside the ditch distracts my eye; I carefully scrape away the muck and leaves to reveal an ancient artifact. It is a glass receptacle in almost perfect condition. The sides are etched and obscured by lichen, but I can still make out markings on the side. It is some form of writing in the Roman alphabet. I am able to decipher the text: *Manor Farm, R. Smillie & Sons, Nettlebed*. Obviously, the folks in the Stone Age liked a little milk with their tea.

I carefully load the relic into my backpack and set off down a mud-strewn path for home. I get no farther than a kilometre when I strike a patch of red mud. My front wheel streaks sideways into a tree root and I hurl straight over the handlebars into the turf. Fortunately, I land on my head—already proven virtually indestructible—and avoid any serious harm, but my bike is in ruins. The front forks are bent backward and the derailleur looks like spaghetti. I estimate the damage at several hundred pounds. With a sigh, I heave it onto my shoulder, careful not to crush my artifact, and limp home.

I awake the next Sunday morning to find the bedroom filled with the short, baleful honks of Canada geese. They reverberate around the room, building to a crescendo that fills me with an incredible yearning for one thing: *foie gras*.

It is mid-month, and Henley is holding its French market in the centre of town. It is a crisp, sunny day, and Linda and I eagerly head out for Falaise Square. As we turn onto Reading Road, we run into the Major out walking Cyprus, his Jack Russell terrier. The Major is in his fifties, with a healthy paunch and a patch of thinning hair plastered to his scalp. We have met several times out walking on Mill Meadows, and he always has some ominous comment on the world in general, uttered through teeth clutching an ancient pipe. "Where are you going in such a great rush—surely it can't be church?"

"We're off to the French market," says Linda.

"*Urgh.*" The Major taps his pipe against the heel of his boot. "Watch out for that lot; they're a bunch of pirates."

Linda and I glance at one another. "You're joking, right?"

The Major clamps his pipe firmly back into his mouth. "We'll see."

About a dozen stalls have set up in the marketplace, and business is brisk. Although I have a list of everything I want for tonight's meal, I can't help doing a run-through of the entire square. A *parfumiere* from Provence has a table full of soaps made from natural ingredients, scented with honeysuckle, lavender, and orange blossom. The smell of langoustine soup from Marseille hangs in the air. Artisans from Aix are offering wicker and cane baskets. M. Maire from Brittany is selling honey, jam, and apple cider. A *charcuterie* has chorizo, *saucisson* with walnuts, and pork sausage with blue cheese on offer. The *épiciere* from Lyon displays half a dozen varieties of homemade mustard, from Dijon to a Provencal mix of pimento and tarragon.

I buy two fresh lamb shanks from the butcher. The grocer has thick juicy carrots, baby potatoes, and—heaven—the first white asparagus of the season. I eagerly fill up my backpack. Before we return home, we make one more stop. The *fromagerie* is a long trailer with sides that fold up to reveal dozens of creamy cheeses on display. The clerk, a young Frenchman with long dreadlocks and a kerchief wrapped around his head, asks my preference. "I would like some of your finest brie," I ask in my best high-school French.

"Of course," he replies, pointing to a forty-centimetre wheel prominently displayed in the case. "I will have my assistant cut you a slice. In the meantime, I would like to show you some of our *chèvre*…" We wander off to the other end of the counter, where he cuts me a slice of delightfully smooth and fresh goat cheese. In the end, I purchase an armload.

When we return home, I unpack the ingredients. Leaving the brie out to breathe, I place the two lamb shanks in a heavy, cast-iron pot and fry them for several minutes in butter and olive oil. Sprinkling on pepper and *herbs de Provence*, I add some whole garlic cloves and shallots. Once everything has browned up nicely, I pour in a cup of white wine, some bay leaves, a sprig of fresh rosemary, and a pinch of salt.

Just as I am placing the pot in the oven, Linda comes down with a load of laundry for the washer. She wrinkles her nose as she passes the kitchen. "What's that smell?"

"The lamb!"

"No, the *other* smell. Didn't you wash your feet today?"

I am so offended by the insinuation that I wait until her back is turned before checking. My socks smell perfectly fine, thank you. *Women*.

We pass the afternoon languidly reading the Sunday papers. Around six, I descend to the kitchen to check on the shanks and add some carrots and the baby potatoes. A wonderful aroma envelopes the room when I lift off the lid.

"Maybe there's a dead rat in the cupboards," says Linda.

"Maybe you need to wait upstairs," I counter. She pours herself a glass of wine, her nose twitching all the while.

By the end of three hours, the meat is so tender that it falls from the bone, I serve it with a bottle of Bordeaux that has been breathing for several hours. Linda forgets the funny smell for the next half-hour, conceding, after several helpings, that it is indeed a wonderful meal.

I clean up the main dishes and go and fetch the cheese plate. By now, the brie has had several hours to warm, and I unwrap the wax paper with great anticipation. Instead of a creamy, runny slice of sublime French cheese, however, I am confronted by a slice of what looks—and smells—like week-old cow stomach. Cursing the cheesemonger's perfidious hide, I carry it out to the garbage bin. I don't know what's worse—being cheated, or the fact that the Major was right.

Oh well, the good news is I can stop scrubbing my feet.

All men love garages, possibly because no woman has ever felt the slightest inclination to decorate one. I can understand; cinder blocks are notoriously unresponsive to taupe paint, and the lack of windows militates against curtains. About the only decorative element that seems to work is a calendar featuring young ladies dressed in as little as possible.

Our garage is a fine example of British architectural design. It is constructed of something reasonably resembling cement, with an assortment of shelves, makeshift workbenches, and untidy piles of leftover tiles gathering dust. The overhead lights look as though they were left over from the bathroom of a Chinese restaurant. The builder of our home has helpfully made the garage too small to actually park a car in, allowing me to claim it for much more important male uses: the storage of nuts and bolts, for instance, none of which fit each other; the chilling of carbonated alcoholic beverages to reasonable consumption temperature; or an area to do experiments, such as ascertaining if an electric carving knife will bisect glass bottles.

I am in the garage today with my meagre set of wrenches and Allen keys, attempting to put my bicycle to rights. I struggle for a few moments until the wrench slips off a bolt and I crack my knuckle sharply against the pedal sprocket. I pull a rag out of my pocket and wrap my hand to staunch the flow of blood, then open the garage door and step outside to curse roundly. The pain gradually subsides, as does my swearing, and by the time Owen emerges for a cigarette, I have calmed down sufficiently to notice he is sporting a rather uncommon hangdog expression on his face.

"Awright?" I ask.

"No. I got scammed," Owen says.

"How so?"

"Them tools—they weren't stolen after all."

I unwrap the rag and am relieved to see that the bleeding has stopped, but the knuckle is beginning to take on a distinctly purplish hue. "That's terrible."

"Bloody right it is—they're just fakes. They buy them by the truckload from Yugoslavia and pawn them off as the real goods."

"The bastards."

"I spent almost a thousand quid on them damn things—nobody's going to buy a phony. What am I supposed to do?"

I shrug. "Rub some dirt on them and sell them as fake antiques."

Owen's eyes light up. "Great idea!"

"Owen, I was just kidding."

"No, it's brilliant. I'll get me a table at a boot sale and fob 'em off!" By now Owen is sufficiently distracted from his own woes to notice my bike. "Whoa, what happened here?" I briefly describe my mishap in the Chilterns. Owen closely examines the damage. "No way you can fix this yourself. You need a repair shop."

"There's a cycle repair shop in Henley?"

"Yep, on Friday Street."

I kick the wrench on the garage floor, pick up the bike, and head off.

Five centuries ago, Friday Street was the rowdy part of town, little more than a muddy lane flanked by stables, pubs, and whorehouses. It had a rich, rotten smell to it, one of life and death and everything jolly in between. London watermen would pull their empty barges hard upstream for three days, their backs and legs toiling, just at the prospect of an overnight stay in its raucous confines. By day, hawkers would tout their loads of barley and wood and pigs destined for market. At night, the shadows would close over the street, and men would steal down to the Anchor pub to gamble their wages and fight and wench.

By all accounts, it's gone downhill since then. The stables and brothels have been converted to whitewashed cottages with exposed timbers and twee little names like The Twiggery. At the end of the street, near Reading Road, is a series of small stores, including the Spoke & Whistle. I had never paid much attention to it before, assuming it was primarily a car parts store, but now, as I carry my bike up to the establishment, I espy various bicycles in the tiny front window.

The interior of the shop is festooned from floor to ceiling with an array of car mats, brake fluids, cleaning compounds, and other automobile paraphernalia, but I also notice a comprehensive array of bicycle accessories along one wall. As I set my bike down on the rough-hewn wooden floor, a man appears from the back storeroom. He is slightly built, perhaps forty years of age, with thinning ginger hair and pale blue eyes that appear to be popping out of his head in surprise. He is wearing a blue work coat that sports several layers of grease and a patch saying *Nigel*.

As an aside, I have never met a Nigel who was born in Canada. It seems that the first thing that everyone does after emigrating from the UK is vow to never name their children Nigel. Thank God. Anyway, this Nigel seems to be a rather decent chap, and nods sympathetically in all the right places as I regale him with the tale of my accident.

When I have finished, he pats my bike on the handlebars. "Good thing it's a Raleigh," he says.

"Why is that?"

"Tough as iron, they are. Could have been a lot worse."

"Can you get parts?"

"No problem." Nigel picks up the bike and carries it into the backroom, where he has a comprehensive repair shop laid out. "We'll have this fixed in no time."

Nigel isn't kidding. As it turns out, he has most of the gear in storage, stripped off salvaged bikes. He pokes through a few cardboard boxes until he finds the necessary parts and then glances at his watch. "Come back in an hour, and she'll be right as rain."

I step outside. With so little time to wait, it almost seems pointless to return home, but the day is a little too raw to wander aimlessly for an hour. I glance at the corner of Friday and Duke streets. There are several junk and antique shops that I have been meaning to investigate. I decide to start with the Henley Antique Centre. The tiny storefront is misleading; as I cross the threshold, it suddenly expands into a large warehouse. The floor is jammed with more than fifty glass-fronted display cases. I am instantly transported back to childhood as I gaze at the treasures within. Here are iron-tipped Maasi spears from East Africa, flintlock pistols from the Civil War, pouting mermaids in porcelain, Devonian ammonites in chalcedony, U-boat captain hats, and a 1/20-scale Black Maria police van with *Wormwood Scrubs* stencilled on the side.

There is much more scattered around the shop out in the open, free for the browser to fondle. I don a black silk top hat and pause to examine a large family Bible perched on a roll-top desk. It is approximately 150 years old and is liberally decorated with steel-engraved illustrations, including a rather saucy rendition of two naked women vainly attempting to escape the Deluge. I flip through the Old Testament, pausing to admire Salome's Dance of the Seven Veils and the various lurid temptations of Sodom and Gomorrah. Boy, they sure knew how to illustrate a Bible back in those days.

Before I have a chance to poke through one quarter of the treasures, an hour has passed, and I reluctantly depart. By the time I get back to the Spoke & Whistle, Nigel has reassembled my bike and even polished off the caked red mud. I pay his fee and thank him profusely, pedalling back home in a fine mood.

I had completely forgotten about George Harrison's architect when Richard calls at the end of the month, but I take down the number and arrange to meet the man a few days later.

David's home is located in the hills overlooking Henley. He is a tall man with a full head of white hair and a relaxed, easygoing personality. We go out to his back garden and sit at a wrought-iron furniture set. He folds himself into a chair and proceeds to relate the circumstances that led to renovating George Harrison's home.

David moved to Henley in the 1960s. At the time, the town was going through a spurt of growth, and architects were in demand. He found work developing new homes and renovating many of the old mansions that dotted the hills. One day, his firm got a call. "Somebody in London wanted an architectural survey of the Friar Park estate," he recalls.

Until the late 1800s, the pastureland north of the town centre was generally referred to as Friar's Field, after a local farmer. In 1895, however, Frank Crisp bought the land and planned out a grand mansion on the hill. When the London solicitor was done, a house of 6100 square metres sat upon twenty-four hectares of landscaped gardens overlooking the town.

"It was a spiky, Victorian Gothic thing made of white stone and brick," says David. "There were three lakes, and a grotto, and a river, and a twenty-foot-high copy of the Matterhorn."

Crisp died and the house eventually became a private school. Over the years, the lakes filled up and the home fell into disarray; in the late 1960s, it was finally put back on the market for sale. "They wanted over £300,000. This was in the days when the average home cost £10,000," says David. "Only a rock star could afford it."

David agreed to do the survey, but almost immediately regretted it. "I drove up to the house and took one look at it and thought, 'What the hell have I gotten myself into?'" The architect was confronted with a massive pile of brick, stone, and overgrown garden. "There weren't even architectural drawings to start with."

Still, he persevered. Although the mansion had suffered decades of neglect, it was still a magnificent building. For two weeks, he measured and documented every room and architectural detail. By the time he was finished, the document was more than an inch thick. He sent it in to the London client and duly received a cheque in payment a month later, cashed it at the bank, and moved on to other work.

It was thus an entirely unsuspecting architect who returned to the office one afternoon to discover that a Mr. Harrison had left a phone message.

"I didn't have any clients named Harrison, so I assumed it was someone in Henley who wanted an addition on their house. I called the number and introduced myself, and the man on the other end of the phone said, 'This is George Harrison, and I've just bought Friar Park. Can you come up here and meet with me?'"

David drove up to the mansion and was met by Harrison at the door. "He said he had liked my work on the survey and wanted me to handle the renovations. And it was as simple as that."

David drew up schedules to repair the leaky roof and install modern heating, plumbing, and electricity, then sat down with the Beatle to discuss alterations. "At first, I thought, my God, what if he wants to do it all in psychedelic colours? But George wasn't like that; he wanted to return everything to the glory of Crisp's original mansion."

Not everything went smoothly. "He had a pedigree cat, a Siamese, or something," David says. "One day, I was up for a meeting, and the cat crawled under my car for a kip. I came out and pulled away, and looked back to see this squashed cat! I thought, Oh no, George will cut me in two!

"I plucked up my courage and went back in and said, 'George, I'm terribly sorry, but I just ran over your cat.' He said, 'That stupid cat! Don't worry about it.'"

Over the next two years, David and Harrison worked hand-in-hand to restore the building. The Beatle loved the task and spent hours writing up lists of details and making sketches. As their time together grew, so did Harrison's trust of the architect. "One evening we sat around drinking a bottle of wine and we started talking. 'Why did you break up?' I asked.

"He replied, 'It had to come sometime. All we did was play John and Paul's songs. Ringo and I wanted to write and play ours too, but they wouldn't let us. We finally got fed up.'"

After the renovations were finished, the two men went their separate ways. David only met the former Beatle once after that, about fifteen years later. "I had gone into the Baskerville Arms pub in Shiplake, and he was there by himself, having a drink. We talked about old days, as though no time had passed. It was very pleasant."

Like everyone else in Henley, David was shocked to hear about the attack by a stalker who had broken into the home and stabbed Harrison. "He came within an inch of being dead."

After I depart from David's home, I cycle back down the hill to the centre of town. Just downstream from the Henley Bridge, across from the Red Lion Hotel, there is a sliver of land along the west bank that has been landscaped and decorated with a few benches. Recently, Henley Council announced that the site would be dedicated as a memorial garden to Harrison's memory. I stop at the park and note that it is the perfect spot for someone stumbling home after a night in the pub to relieve their bladder. I recall David's words when I asked him about the tribute. "Personally, if someone had dedicated this informal urinal to me, I would have considered it quite a backhander, but Henley Council seems unfazed. That's politicians for you."

Certainly, there is nothing particularly reminiscent of George about the place that I can conjure up: no pliant sitar notes wafting in the breeze, no gently weeping guitars, not even a walrus paddling about in the river. Or was that Paul? I am about to give up when the clouds part and a beautiful ray of light cascades down to the shore. Well then, here comes the sun. It's all right. I get back on my bike and pedal home a happy man.

9

APRIL

'Tis the Season to Gossip

For some reason that eludes me, Henley traditionally celebrates April Fools' Day by hanging hundreds of flower baskets around town. Apparently, this started some years ago with the launch of the "Bloomin' Britain" campaign, an annual affair where communities run a comb through their collective thatch and generally spruce up the town by evicting spiky-haired beggars and planting begonias. Henley, of course, studiously ignored the entire process until neighbouring Marlow won first place. Since then, they have hung bushels of begonias, buttercups, and bleeding hearts from every street lamp, garbage truck, and passed-out drunkard in order to win the top prize.

I am on my way back from Woolworth's with a sheaf of printer paper when I spot what I first assume to be a disemboweled Martian hanging from a lamppost. It is a fibre pot containing purple petunias and blood-red pelargoniums bulging out of a bed of bright green lacy fern. I am trying to decide the most opportune time to sneak by and ignite it when Edwina, dressed in her best Sunday clothes, approaches. She is wearing an immense spring bonnet affixed with feathers and silk butterflies that bob about on tiny steel coils. "How do you like my chapeau?" she asks.

"It's as pretty as a hanging basket," I reply. "What brings you out on this fine spring morning?"

Edwina leans forward, her mouth twitching in delighted outrage. "Haven't you heard the latest?"

In fact, the tale had been making the rounds for the last few days. Gyles Groodey, a local politician, has left his wife of long standing for a divorcée. "Do you think it will affect his chances of re-election?" I ask.

Edwina's eyebrows rise in mock outrage. "We *do* have standards in this town, you know." I ponder this as she and her butterflies bob off.

Really, the British are nuts. You wouldn't know it from a casual glance—what other nation considers wool socks as lingerie?—but they truly are demented. As I continue on my way, I wonder if it's contagious. I arrive home and head up to my office with the paper. I reload the printer then stare out the window at the fluffy clouds scudding by, trying to decide how best to spice this latest news up in my diary.

It is precisely that moment when I notice the spy peering at me from a window in an apartment block across the street. He is bald, with thick black glasses and a sinister comb-over. All I can see is his head, which is pointed directly at my house and moving neither left nor right. I am beginning to wonder if it is a real head at all—perhaps it's just a dummy noggin put out to scare off Jehovah's Witnesses—but no, it just moved, and besides, a head on a pike would just attract religious nuts.

How long has he been watching? I start to search back through my memory for various personal moments that may have been less than outstanding, such as the time a few weeks ago I sat out on a patio chair in nothing but pink shorts in order to expose my pale hide to the few rays of sun that had managed to penetrate the ubiquitous March clouds. I cringe. No doubt he has made a running chronicle of all the empty bottles I have carted, clinking and clanking, out to the garbage bin late at night under cover of darkness. What if he just makes something up and feeds it to the press? "Reliable sources confirm that Mr. Cope has been secretly entertaining goats in late-night feta cheese orgies." That sort of thing can give a writer a reputation, you know.

Linda passes the doorway with a load of laundry. I hiss to catch her attention.

"What's wrong?"

I pull her behind the curtain. "Look across the street. Do you see the bald guy?"

"What about him?"

"He's *spying* on me."

"Are you nuts?"

"No! I've been watching him for weeks now. He's definitely spying."

"Don't be silly." Linda puts down the basket of laundry and waves out the window. Bald Guy waves back. "He's just a harmless old man. I see him walking his wiener dog every morning when I'm driving to work."

"Don't wiener dogs come from East Germany? He could be retired Stasi."

Linda sighs. "I know what the problem is—you've got too much idle time on your hands." She takes me by the collar and drags me downstairs and out the front door. She opens the trunk of our car and lifts out a brand new spade.

I stare at it with deep suspicion. "What do you want me to do with this?"

Adjacent to our front walk is a patch of dirt and weeds, about a metre wide and three metres long, which has all the charm of a mass gravesite. Linda points at it. "I want you to make a garden."

A lavender plant, neglected for the last several years, squats in scraggly fashion against the wall. "There's already a garden there," I protest.

"No, a real garden. With flowers and herbs."

"But there might be worms and things in there."

"Think positive. I heard on the news last week that someone dug up three thousand gold Roman coins in their garden."

"Don't be ridiculous. I hardly think I'm going to find anything valuable *there*."

"I know for a fact you will."

"How so?"

Linda hands me the spade. "I buried your wallet last night."

Bowing to the inevitable, I don my wellies and a sturdy pair of leather gloves and begin to dig. For the first few moments I entertain dark thoughts, but then an inspiration brightens my mood: perhaps I'll find a bony hand clutching silver pennies. I have a few false starts over bottle caps, but sadly, no skeletal remains. Rather, my spade clinks dully against a maze of roots from the nearby mountain ash tree. Over the course of half an hour, I manage to wrestle out a string of knotty wood about the size of a rat's intestines. At this rate, it will be September before I even have it tilled. I ponder going back in and admitting defeat, but I worry I may never get my wallet back. This calls for drastic action. I ring Alan's doorbell.

After a long pause, the door opens. "Awright?" I ask.

Alan is dressed in Garfield pajamas. "Not really."

"What's wrong?"

Alan's face takes on a pained expression, and he tentatively rubs his stomach. "I don't know, I just feel punk."

"You know what you need? A little fresh air and excitement."

Alan's face brightens slightly. "What you got in mind?"

"A treasure hunt."

"Really? I *love* treasure hunts."

"Great. Put on some workboots and we'll get started."

A few minutes later, Alan joins me outside. "Where are we off to?"

I point to the patch. "Right here."

"What, *there*? Who told you there was buried treasure?"

"I have it on the highest authority." I hand him the spade. "Here, you start."

I pull out a lawn chair from the garage and sit down sufficiently far away to avoid being inadvertently struck, but close enough to supervise. Under my skillful direction, Alan lifts away the weeds and most of the crab grass. "Isn't this fun?" I say.

Alan looks up from his labours, a streak of sweat running down his face. "I'd rather be painting."

I'm impressed, but not enough to take over shovelling. "I didn't know you were a painter."

"Not really. In fact, I'm awful."

"Don't be so harsh. I'll bet you're no worse than dreadful."

Alan pauses in his digging. "Thanks."

"No, I'm serious. Why don't you show me something you've done?"

"I ripped them all up."

"Well then, why don't you paint something new and I'll decide if it's good or not."

Alan's eyebrows assume a dubious arc. "How do I know you won't say that it's good just to be nice?"

"Dig some more of this bloody garden for me and I promise I'll be brutally honest."

"It's a deal." Alan sets to his task and the dirt flies. Before I even have a chance to finish my first beer, he has most of the garden tilled.

"Hold it," I command.

"What?"

"There." The corner of my wallet is sticking out near the wall. Alan pulls it out. "*This* is the buried treasure?"

"Yep." I check the wallet. Except for two gumballs in the change purse, it is empty. I give one to Alan. "Here's your half of the loot."

Alan pops it into his mouth. "Gosh, thanks."

"You're welcome." I point to his pajamas. "Now, put on some trousers and I'll buy you a pint."

This gardening isn't so tough, after all. In fact, all of this agricultural activity is quite stimulating, and the following day I decide to go for a run. I am jogging along the path adjacent to the Thames, my mind blissfully absent from all things topiary, when I suddenly notice movement in a pale blue Mercedes sedan parked in a car lot overlooking the river. The windows are foggy, but there is definitely a lady's shoe resting vertically on the rear window ledge. The shoe, in fact, is a black stiletto high heel, and it is attached to a rather shapely naked calf. Presumably, the calf hooks up to an equally unclad thigh somewhere within, but I am too modest to run up and check. Besides, judging from the pronounced rocking of the car, whoever is in there with her is obviously large and robust, and—just a guess—not too amenable to distractions at this moment.

There are two passion pits in the vicinity, this one beside the River & Rowing Museum, and the other adjacent to the train station. Both have the advantages of being close to the workplace and nearly deserted during midday. This is ideal if, after a few too many lunch-hour pints, you decide that the best way to work off the excess alcohol is a brief, vigorous round of fornication in the back seat of a company car with the miniskirt from accounting.

Of course, if you choose the River & Rowing venue, you risk being seen by anyone passing by. Although the pair are undoubtedly oblivious to my presence, I do the proper British thing and hum a merry tune and glance with fascination at a semi-submerged fibreglass boat on the far shore until I have passed by some ten metres. I then swivel my head a full one hundred eighty degrees, but all I can see for my efforts is a pate of ash-blonde hair periodically tapping against the side window. By the time I return from the far point of my run, they have gone; save for a forlorn latex condom being inspected by a seagull, there is no evidence of their presence.

When I arrive back home, a box that Linda has ordered from a garden catalogue is sitting on the doorstep. I scoop it up and rush inside to the living room. I rip it open and a large blob of dirt spills out upon the dining-room table. There, resplendent in a fat little pile, is an assortment of 'Stargazer,' 'Princess Delight,' and 'Moonbeam' magic bulbs—£50 worth, in all. If the government ever wanted to balance the budget, they could do worse than muscling into this racket.

I take the package outside and sit on the stoop. The bulbs come with instructions on how deep and far apart each should be planted. I rip these up and throw them away—mustn't be too Anglo-Saxon about this, mustn't we—then get down to the business of digging in the dirt. I have purchased three bags of decomposed manure, which I work into the soil as I go along. I follow a plan that Alan and I carefully drafted on the back of a pub napkin the previous evening. It has been somewhat revised due to a large lager stain, but this is a small impediment.

"*Oy*, whatcha got there?"

Owen, ubiquitous fag in hand, is peering over my shoulder. I proudly show off my prizes. "Dahlias, lilies, and irises."

"*Ooh*. Very nice."

"Thanks. Do you garden?"

"No time. I got me a new boat."

I shudder to think. "I hope it's a rubber dinghy."

"No way. We're talkin' sixteen-foot fibreglass hull with a hundred and fifty horses. This baby really flies."

"What do you need all that power for? You're not allowed to go over ten knots on the river."

"Sod the river. I'm taking it down to the English Channel. Maybe continue all the way up the Seine to Paris."

I have a vision of Mr. Magoo in a motor boat. "You can't be serious."

"Yep. Gonna take it on a *real* booze cruise to France."

"Do you have a name for it yet?"

"Nope. Got any ideas?"

"How about the *Titanic*?"

Owen stubs his cigarette and returns to work, leaving me to finish my gardening. I idly wonder if the lilies will be up in time to make a wreath.

Good Friday arrives mid-month. It is a fine spring day, and I decide to go for a bike ride. I pull my cycle from the garage and am pumping up the front tire when I notice Owen in the adjacent marina parking lot carefully attaching a boat trailer to his car. The boat gleams in the sun, the white fibreglass hull polished to a brilliant glow. In spite of my worries, I join him to admire the craft. "It's beautiful."

Owen puffs up with pride. "I paid eight thousand quid for it. If the wife finds out, it's divorce number three."

"You're really taking it out on the Channel?"

"You bet." Owen glances at his watch. "Me and Kim should be in Southampton by three, and France by five."

"Well, be careful."

Owen flicks his cigarette in a graceful arch over the boat's petrol tank. "Careful's my middle name."

I bid him farewell and start up the hill toward Reading Road, where I encounter a procession led by a man dressed in archaic robes and carrying a large wooden cross. Henley is generally not a place for superstition; there is little truck hereabouts for palmistry and tarot reading, and bylaws strictly prohibit incorporeal spirits from wandering about public edifices. Anglicanism, of course, is another matter, and even though the following throng is bereft of cat o' nine tails, a festive mood fills the air. I cheerily wave to J.C. as I pedal by, noting that, except for the fact that his crown of thorns is plastic and he is wearing hiking boots, everything else appears authentic. But that's the Anglican way, isn't it? Cut the passion out of the Passion but throw in a bit of a ramble.

I stop in Market Square in order to decide which way to go. Shall I head west, up the Chilterns, or how about east, to Crazies Hill? The Major strolls by as I consult my topographic map. "Beautiful day for a ride," he notes.

"It is. I haven't decided where to go yet, though."

"In that case, you must go see the toad crossing."

"What a splendid idea! I'll stop by on my way to Ratty and Mole's cottage."

The Major taps his pipe on the heel of his boot. "I'm serious." It seems that amorous amphibians in search of a mate were getting flattened under lorries as they tried to make their way across the highway leading to Marlow. In France, this would be an invitation to set up a barbecue grill, but for some reason or other they thought it necessary here to put in an underpass instead. "The hard part was training them to use it," says the Major.

I can imagine; we're talking about a horny toad here, the last thing they want to do is take a course in ditch navigation. I finally agree to go have a look, however. "Where is it?"

"Near the turnoff for Fawley," he says. "You can't miss it."

I thank the Major and head off. Traffic through town is fairly light, and I reach the main road to Marlow relatively unmolested. I head north, my eyes peeled. The Major has warned me that the toad crossing is fairly innocuous, merely a steel grating across the road. I finally find it after about three passes up and down the road, and I have to agree, it's certainly nothing much to write home to Granny about; I've seen sexier drainage ditches. In fact, I would be disappointed in a major league way were it not for the most amazing sight directly across the road; the ground beneath a large stand of mature beech trees, extending for several acres, is literally awash with tiny bluebells.

The toad crossing forgotten, I enter the beeches and proceed up a sandy path into the middle of the forest, until the sound of traffic fades to a gentle murmur. I sit upon an ancient, white-washed stump and gaze at the scene all around me. Far above, the leaves undulate in the breeze, their shiny green surfaces reflecting the light like sparkles on a fast-flowing stream. The strong, grace-ful trunks descend to the forest floor, where low green vegetation mixes with the bluebells to form a living carpet of emerald and sapphire. Butterflies and insects dance in the sunbeams that pen-etrate the canopy above.

I would have lingered for hours were it not for the fact that I am sitting in something sticky. I stand up and realize that the whitewash on the stump is still wet, and I have managed to create a decorative bum pattern on my riding shorts. As I try to brush it off, I step backward into a patch of nettles. My ankles are gripped by a raw burning sensation and a red rash appears on my skin. I leap back on my bike and head toward the nearest pharmacy, my legs aflame.

They were brilliant bluebells, though.

By Saturday morning, the itching has gone down sufficiently that I am once again mobile. I walk out to the front steps with my coffee and gaze absently down upon my garden. I immediately notice that something has changed overnight; the dahlia tubers appear to be bulging out of the ground. Puzzled, I lean over and examine them more closely, this time correctly identifying the brown, oblong objects as feline poop.

Nicky, a young woman who works at the same business as Owen, emerges from the office door with her morning tea. "Cats love soft ground," she explains. "I had that problem with my neighbour's moggie."

"What did you do?" I ask.

"Got some slate pebble from the garden centre."

"How does that stop them?"

"Scratches up their little arses. Keeps the weeds down, too."

The workings of the universe truly are a mystery. I finish my coffee just as Linda comes out the front door, all dressed up. "Where are you off to?" I ask.

"You're taking me to lunch."

"Lovely. Where?"

"We're going to the St. George and the Dragon."

I have always had a keen interest in things George, slayer of mythical beasts, protector of virgins, and patron saint of a country that didn't exist when he was alive. In fact (or whatever passes for fact under the circumstances), George was a Roman tribune in the army of Diocletian, a third-century-A.D. emperor known for his persecution of Christians. George, a Christian himself, complained about this unfair treatment to the emperor, who chopped his head off for being so cheeky. Apparently, the dragon-slaying and virgin-protecting business was added to his CV at a later date by troubadours accompanying Richard the Lionheart on the Crusades. Thanks to their less-than-sober accounts of his legend, George was saddled with the dragon myth.

A double-sided signboard marks the St. George and the Dragon pub in Wargrave, just south of Henley. On one side is a fierce dragon standing amidst the litter of empty armour, ogling a comely maiden with the salacious glee that only a serpent can muster. On the other side is the same serpent, now very dead. George, clad in golden armour, rests one foot upon its belly. His right arm holds his lance high, while his left clasps a mug of ale as the princess gazes lovingly into his eyes. Well, if that doesn't whet the appetite, I don't know what will.

The interior of the pub has recently been refurbished, with whitewashed walls and a freshly sanded plank floor. It is obviously a very old building, and the oak beams, painted a glossy black, meander across the low ceiling like thick, black snakes. We order wild boar sausage and mash; it is a hearty, good meal, and our plates are soon picked cleaner than the suits of armour that lay near the dragon's lair.

By the time we return home, it is mid-afternoon. I am rather surprised to see Owen unhitching a decidedly empty boat trailer. "Back so soon? I thought you were going to spend the whole weekend out on the high seas."

Owen glances vaguely skyward. "Well, you know, bit of a change of plans." I am about to ask the whereabouts of his boat, when Owen glances at his watch. "Gotta run." He stubs out his cigarette and beats a hasty retreat.

Just then, Kim walks around the corner. I point to Owen's receding backside. "What's wrong with him?"

"He sank his boat."

"Oh my God. Is everyone all right?"

"Oh yeah, right as rain."

"How did it happen?"

"He ran it into an oil tanker."

I shake my head. "I told him not to try and cross the English Channel."

Kim snorts. "It was docked in Southampton Harbour when he ran into it. They hauled him out with a big hook."

I can't help but think he should have spent the Easter weekend just hanging around, like J.C.

A few days later, I drop into Mr. Trowbridge's to pick up some ground meat. I casually ask the butcher if he intends to vote for any of the candidates in the upcoming election.

"I'd like to shoot a few, that's what I'd like to do."

I am eyeing my ground meat dubiously when Teddy pulls up on his Henley-Davidson. He lifts a *Standard* out from his hamper. "Have you seen this morning's paper? Lord Hambleden's put his manor up for sale."

I take the paper from Teddy's hands and read the lead story. Apparently, the heir to the W.H. Smith fortune is selling about 607 hectares and forty-five properties for something in the neighbourhood of £30 million.

Trowbridge shakes his head in disbelief. "Why on earth would he do such a thing?"

"I hear he's going through a divorce," says Teddy. "Maybe he needs the money to settle it."

"Too bad, it's brilliant," says Trowbridge. He turns to me. "Take my advice, young man, see it before some rich American buys it and throws up a gate."

I take him at his word. Hauling out my trusty cycle, I head north along the Marlow Road until I arrive once again at the toad crossing. Instead of stopping for amorous amphibians, however, I turn west and head toward Fawley. For the first kilometre, the narrow twisting lane is bounded by sheep fields and forests covered in bluebells. An immense oak, its trunk about a metre across, has been felled across the road by a recent storm; fortunately, someone has cut it into sections and rolled it out of the way. Farther along, two rows of hawthorne trees have bent over the road to form a long, dark tunnel.

I am enjoying myself immensely until I arrive at the end of the hawthorne trees and discover that the road has taken a turn for the vertical; I have been on bobsled runs that are less steep. My ass becomes numb just looking at it. I pedal valiantly for a further hundred metres before I am forced to dismount and push my bike the rest of the way.

Finally, I reach the top. I pause at the crest of the Chilterns amid a beech and evergreen forest. Clouds roll by, scraping the tops of the trees. A tall spruce has been hit by lightning, tearing the crown off and splitting the bark all the way to the ground with a black, sooty scar. According to my trusty topographic map, about two kilometres north of me is the Luxters Farm Vineyard and Brewery, marked with a large blue star. I follow the twisting lanes until I come to a gate announcing my destination.

The farm is a quadrangle of low stone cottages surrounding a forecourt. The owner of the establishment is more than happy to pour me a pint of bitter. It is cold and refreshing, and I sip it with pleasure as he explains how he gave up a career in maritime law in the City in order to become a vintner and brewer in rural Buckinghamshire. They have one hectare of Sylvaner grapes, from which they produce eight different wines, including a sparkling rosé. I take my pint outside and sit down beneath a lilac tree filled with purple blossoms and unpack my lunch. I am joined by two black Labradors who are more than eager to share my BLT and beer. When I finish, they escort me down the road, racing through the fields and startling pheasants into flight.

I continue on my way eastward, descending the Chilterns into a wide, gently undulating valley. I turn south toward the river and cycle at a leisurely pace for two kilometres or so until I come to a small signpost marked *Hambleden*. A short, cobbled path leads to around three dozen stone cottages arranged around the tiny central square. It's strangely quiet. In fact, the busiest spot seems to be the graveyard by St. Mary the Virgin Church, where a retired couple from Heathrow are resting on a bench.

"We heard about this place on the news, so we thought we'd take a look," says the husband. He is wearing a baseball cap and carries a camcorder around his neck. "Can't say as I'd want to buy it, though—looks like a lot of upkeep."

I am about to head out when I spot Alan's Lotus Elice. The bright blue car is sitting in front of the local pub. I lock my bike up to a light standard and wander in, but, except for two aged men in the garden, it is empty. I am about to return to my journey when I spy a lone figure atop a nearby hill, sitting on a portable stool in front of an easel. The hill is in the middle of a pasture, overlooking the village. Taking a cow path, I climb the hill toward Alan. He is concentrating so deeply that he doesn't notice my approach. "Hullo," I say.

"Oh! Hullo. What are you doing here?"

"I rode out to see if Hambleden was worth buying. I'm told it needs a lot of upkeep, though." I point to the easel. "How's your work going?"

"Brilliant."

"Mind if I take a look?"

"Actually, I do." The easel is equipped with a pair of doors that fold over the canvas. Alan closes them. "If you don't mind, I'd prefer to show it when it's done."

"No! Not at all." I slowly turn to go. "Well, I'll be seeing you then."

Alan waves goodbye. "Cheers."

I have to admit I'm a little put out, being the inspiration for Alan to return to the genre and all, but it's his perfect right to show it to whomever he wants, the ungrateful bastard. Nobody can accuse me of having a thin skin, although I have to admit it is rather sore in certain parts by the time I reach home.

Every year, toward the latter part of April, Henley celebrates Dusty Springfield Day. Not *officially*, of course. Somehow, the town council still hasn't quite gotten around to honouring a soul-singing lesbian with a weakness for bouffant wigs, but that doesn't seem to bother her legions of loyal fans. I'm not a devotee of Dusty's, but she *is* buried here, and I must confess I'm a big fan of English graveyards. First of all, they're always very amenable to contemplation, being by design rather quiet and peaceful; one can cogitate upon the big picture without being distracted by the inhabitants. They are also generally well decorated in the earth tones, with buttery stone markers, verdant moss, and weeping willows the colour of lime. Finally, they aren't overly oppressive, bulging to the brim with grey stone sepulchres, but open and grassy, filled with light and soft shadow.

I especially like St. Mary's graveyard. It is small and comfy, bounded on three sides by rows of whitewashed alms houses, their bright blue doors flanked by pots of chrysanthemums. The inscriptions on most of the sandstone grave markers have long since weathered away, leaving the inhabitants to rest in anonymous peace. Except for Dusty's, of course. Her grave marker, a simple slab, has been carved from impermeable granite and set flush with the ground. It states simply, "Dusty Springfield, OBE, 1939-1999." When I arrive, two fans, a man and a woman, are tending the site, arranging displays of yellow roses, framed photographs, and plush teddy bears around the marker. The woman, with hair dyed bright blue, smiles as I walk past. The man ignores me, standing silently at vigil, with only the occasional reverential twisting of his nose ring to reveal his contemplative state of mind.

A wooden bench has been placed some distance from Dusty's site. It is painted in brown enamel and inscribed, "Bob and Mary, who enjoyed this spot, invite you to linger." It is not a particularly warm spring day, but the walls around the yard cut the northern wind, and I take up Bob and Mary's invitation and sit on the bench. The couple soon leaves.

Alone, I drift into reverie until something nips me on the ankle. I shriek in proper graveyard fashion, which causes the kitten beneath the bench to bolt for the nearest ivy bush in panic.

She is perhaps ten months old, a brown Siamese with bright blue eyes. It takes several minutes for me to coax her out, but when she finally emerges, she decides that I am a suitable playmate. She is wearing a leather collar with a blue, heart-shaped locket announcing her name to be Kookai. She takes me on a tour of her domain, grabbing hold of my shoelace when I head in the wrong direction, rewarding me with a copious amount of fur upon my trouser leg when I stop at the right destination. Whenever my attention wanders, she lets out a sound that is a mix of purr and growl to let me know where I should be properly focused. I have no catnip to pay for the tour, but she is content to accept a belly rub in compensation.

I bid adieu to Kookai and Dusty and head back out onto the street, turning my attention toward the site of the day's major festivities, the Queen's Head. This aptly named pub, located on Duke Street, is heaving to the sound of "Son of a Preacher Man" as impersonators in sequined ball gowns and big, big wigs belt out the tunes. Cigarettes, clutch purses, and sparkle lipstick are rife. Anybody not dressed in Mary Quant is turned away at the door and must bribe the bouncer at the back with a joint to get in.

I spot David through the window and wave to catch his attention. The *Standard* reporter has a word with the manager who nods and lets me in. I buy David a round and observe him manfully trying to write a story while having his bum pinched by a transvestite in six-inch heels.

I endure about an hour of this before I note that my skin is taking on the texture of a kipper from all the second-hand smoke. I bid adieu to a stevedore in pink taffeta and head back to Hart Street. The main drag is lined with half a dozen watering holes, ranging from the Catherine Wheel pub to Latrino's nightclub. The latter is decorated in traditional Tex-Mex barn wood with steer horns and tin roofing over the roughed-in bar. Country and western music blasts out of speakers the size of Volkswagens and the menu features such delicacies as armadillo cheese melts and bull testicles.

As I near Latrino's, a door slams open and a woman and man appear on the sidewalk ahead. She is slapping her arms and legs as though being consumed by a swarm of imaginary bees. I stare in bewilderment for a moment until a familiar tune carries out from the bar into the street—"The Macarena." The song is one of those completely pointless salsa tunes, but one cannot deny there is a certain charm to watching a group of seventeen-year-old Brazilian girls in thong bikinis performing the dance. It loses a little something, however, when a pudgy hairstylist in a pink tube top starts wiggling a pair of chunky thighs. Nonetheless, her male companion feels sufficiently stimulated to grab various nether portions, which results in an impressive elbow to his nose. Two club bouncers appear from within and attempt conflict mediation without losing their sunglasses. The girl responds with several phrases never uttered by Emily Brontë and knocks the rear-view mirror off a car. An enthusiastic crowd gathers to enjoy the festivities, chanting encouragement.

The Thames Valley Police soon arrive to join the fun. Once upon a time, police patrolled on foot, until the TVP had the brilliant idea to equip its force with tiny white hatchback Rovers painted bright yellow and orange. Not exactly intimidating; in fact, if they ever wanted to make a few spare quid, all they'd have to do is play "Pop Goes the Weasel" and everyone would come round to buy an ice cream cone.

The woman takes one look at the car and bursts into a stream of profanity. The coppers get out of the car. They are dressed in the traditional black Bobby hats with a brass button on top, as well as thick belts holding flashlights, latex gloves, handcuffs, truncheons, and whatnot. They order the crowd to disperse. Two lads respond by repositioning some street furniture through a plate-glass window and then fleeing toward the river. The police hop back into their ice cream vans and roar off in hot pursuit. Meanwhile, several of the revellers from the Queen's Head have joined the festivities and entertain the remaining crowd with Dusty's version of Burt Bacharach's "This Girl's in Love with You."

Say what you like about this town, but boy, they sure know how to have fun.

10
MAY

Time to Vote

It is May Day, and Henley's citizens are celebrating in the dullest manner possible, by voting. It's not as though they don't have alternatives, you know. In Paris, they riot; Moscow trundles out immense ICBMs; and Romans go on strike and head for the beach. At the very least, they could take up Mr. Trowbridge's suggestion and shoot a few politicians.

It is a wet, blustery day, which has at least cleared Market Place Square of skateboarders. In fact, the only surly, underemployed locals lurking around are the candidates standing near the front door of town hall, directly below the official town crest. Henley's crest is a good example of why heraldic manufacturers should all be awarded one-way tickets to Ulan Bator. At the centre is a blue shield with a gold *H* wearing a crown. Not in itself so bad, but the letter is being supported by a bull and a griffin, each one wearing some sort of yodelling horn on a necklace. A pair of crossed oars and a knight's helmet rising out of a fog bank are positioned above the shield. Finally, the fringe has been tarted up with various gew-gaws and the town motto, *Semper communitas,* which, according to my rough translation, means "always gossip."

The candidates are decked out in dark blue suits and identical smiles, their only distinguishing feature the various lapel rosettes indicating party affiliation. As I ascend the steps, one of the blue suits breaks out of the pack and rushes forward to shake my hand. "Are you here to vote today, sir?"

"Sorry, I'm not a local citizen," I reply. He drops my hand faster than a glove salesman at a leper colony, and I enter the building relatively unimpeded.

The town hall has all the warmth of a mausoleum. I advance to the council chamber where four clerks in various stages of disinterest are sitting in the otherwise deserted room. One glances up briefly from her tabloid newspaper to ask if I need any help, but once she realizes that I am only there to look, not vote, I am ordered to leave, lest democracy be undermined by my eyeballs. I retreat from their bureaucratic gaze before frostbite sets in.

I am writing down notes for my diary as I exit the town hall, which is a blunder, as one of the lurking politicians mistakes me for a journalist and rushes over. Andrew is a local businessman running for county council. He is a compact man with a sharp set of teeth. "Can you believe the mess they made of this Market Place? They closed off a major arterial route and shoppers are going to other towns—they say it's too much aggravation coming here!"

I jot this down. "So, you're saying that Henley is up the Thames without a paddle?"

It turns out Andrew has an even sharper talent for reversing at high speed. "Oh, no! It's a very nice town, and everyone gets on with each other. Did you know there are more service organizations per head of population than any other town in the country?" It certainly has more boozehounds, but I let that that observation slide as Andrew barrels along. "It builds on what the town recognizes—people helping each other. There are dozens and dozens of organizations."

I stop writing, and Andrew's verbal diarrhea gradually abates to the point where I can get a word in edgewise. "You can't deny that the development caused problems."

"Okay, the Market Place did split the town in two. I just hope everything settles down."

I spot Derek from the marina as he marches by on his way to the police station. I bid farewell to Andrew and head off in pursuit. "Awright?" I call out.

Derek rubs the back of his neck in frustration. "Bloody kids."

"What's wrong?"

"They stole another boat last night."

"*Another* one?"

"The third this month. They sneak in at night and hot-wire the battery. The little beggars hung the last one up on the weir at Hambleden. Kim spent half a week repairing the diesel."

I recall being woken up several nights ago by some noise, but it had been pitch black outside and I had gone back to bed. "I promise I'll keep an eye peeled."

Derek turns toward the station. "Thanks. If I ever get my hands on them…" I leave Derek to his ruminations.

Picking up some wine at the bottle shop, I head for home. I arrive just as Alan emerges from his front door. "How's your painting going?" I ask.

"Brilliant."

"Great. I can't wait to see it."

"Too late. It's already gone."

"You *sold* it?"

"Not exactly. I entered it into a competition."

It turns out that the town of Acton, located east of Henley, mounts an adjudication of amateur works during its annual art fair. I'm impressed and say so.

"Well, we'll see," adds Alan, perhaps suddenly aware of the chance he's taken. "There's lots of talented people out there. We'll see."

The following weekend is the first spring Bank Holiday in Britain, and Henley is greeted with beautiful, sunny weather. This, of course, fills the locals with no end of suspicion. As I walk along the riverbank, I pass a long row of anchored boats. Every few minutes, one of their residents sticks his nose out of the main cabin and glances balefully at the blue sky, wondering what awful thing he must have done in life to deserve such a brilliant day.

I am on my way to see how preparations are coming for the annual Henley Royal Regatta. Even though it isn't held until July, the week-long event will attract more than one hundred entries and two hundred thousand visitors per day. Construction of the temporary river course, viewing stands, competitor tents, and hospitality areas must begin several months in advance.

As I cross Henley Bridge, I spot a long procession of white tents sprouting from the green fields adjacent to the Leander Club. I can't even begin to guess how much acreage is being covered by the temporary structures, but it must run into hundreds of thousands of square metres.

I suppose I could just look it up in the *Guide to Henley Regatta & Reach*, a book written by Teddy's friend Michael Jones. The Henley native has been messing about on the river his entire life as a rower and supporter of the sport and has put together an idiosyncratic compendium of facts and trivia concerning all things racy.

According to Jones's book, for instance, the official crest of the Leander Club sports a pink hippo. Pimm's, the official drink of the regatta, is an icy mix of gin, lemon, cucumber, apples, and oranges, topped with a sprig of mint. About thirty thousand pints are consumed each year.

The regatta course itself—officially set at one mile, five hundred fifty yards long—is the primary reason Henley was chosen in the first place; it is one of the few places on the meandering Thames where the river remains relatively straight for so long a distance.

I enter into the grounds and make my way into one of the tents. It is a very spacious affair, perhaps twelve metres wide and sixty metres long, and it is filled with giant steel racks. "They're for holding the sculls and oars," explains a security guard. I thank him and proceed on, mindful not to be run over by the construction lorries that criss-cross the fields. Officials in orange vests wander about, demarcating plots of land into parking lots, stewards' enclosures, and food areas. I begin to get an inkling of the sheer vastness of the undertaking as I watch a score of portable latrines being placed in a seemingly endless line. Champagne, I conclude, must be a very powerful purgative.

As I exit the grounds onto Remenham Road, I spot Peter's estate wagon in Teddy's driveway. The pair are dressed in hunting gear—brown canvas vests, high-topped wellies, and wide-brimmed hats—and are busy loading a picnic basket into the rear seat of the car. "Going on a hunt?" I ask.

"Are you daft?" retorts Peter. "It's May. There's no hunting in May."

I point to their outfits. "What's with the gear then?"

"We're going to London," replies Teddy.

I am about to compliment them on their excellent choice of city clothing when a woman appears from the back entrance to Barn Cottage. She is tall and blonde, perhaps forty, with a sharply sculpted chin.

"May I introduce my niece, Julia?" says Teddy. She extends her hand, and I shake it.

Julia has a strong, farmwoman's grip. "A pleasure to meet you," she says in the kind of accent you associate with cucumber sandwiches. "Would you care to sign our petition?"

"What petition is that?"

Julia digs a clipboard out of the car and hands it to me. "It's against the government's ban on fox hunting."

I take the clipboard from Julia like she is handing me a land mine, which, in effect, she is. Banning fox hunting is one of those no-win issues that have gripped the country over the last several years, dividing people into vermin huggers on one side and mammal mutilators on the other. "I'm not quite sure I understand why you're protesting," I say.

"Blair doesn't understand the role of hunting in the countryside," says Teddy of their beloved PM. "It's the fabric of the culture. The government has absolutely no idea how important it is to so many people."

Adds Julia, "I am bitterly, positively opposed to the law, and I will gladly disobey it and go to prison."

Well, just the sort of thing I love to sign, then. "Is it really that bad?"

"That's why we're going to protest against it," says Teddy. "Julia thinks there's going to be a million people there."

I turn to Peter. "I didn't realize you loved hunting that much."

He shakes his head. "I hate it. I'm just driving these two into London so I can pick up some cheap plonk in town."

Teddy rolls his eyes. "See if I ever ask *you* to a grouse hunt again."

"I shall be most pleased," Peter says. "The last time I attended, you shot my dog."

Two large Labradors race around the corner of Barn Cottage. While Julia is momentarily distracted loading them into the rear, I pitch the clipboard back into the car and help Teddy into the front seat. I wave cheerily as they drive off, admonishing them to give it their most obnoxious enthusiasm.

By the time I return to town and fetch Linda, the May Fair is well underway. Instead of a maypole, the town has opted for another traditional celebration, a performance by the Amazing Ray, who is scheduled to take a fifteen-metre dive off a portable ladder into a large sponge bale at 3:30 PM. It's still half an hour to launch time, so we decide to tour the grounds. The meadow is ringed with an assortment of charity booths, peanut brittle stalls, and games of chance. For half a quid, you can pick your favourite stuffed animal by knocking a coconut off a tin can. Winnie the Pooh is very popular, although the coral snake, one of the most venomous animals on the face of the earth, seems to be a local favourite. I blame video games.

I bump into Richard, who is taking pictures of the fair. I ask him how the election went.

Apparently, Gyles Groodey got turfed. Richard shakes his head: "I can't believe this town."

Precisely on the half-hour, the master of ceremonies enters a large enclosure surrounding the ladder and announces that Amazing Ray will perform his death-defying leap as soon as he can be located. A search proves fruitless, however, and the emcee must press his assistant Trevor into performing. The hapless man clambers awkwardly up the ladder, slipping and dangling as he ascends. Once he reaches the top, the emcee asks the crowd for the countdown, but Trevor is reluctant to take the plunge, prefer-ring to drop his trousers to the audience below. Finally, Trevor steps into space and hurtles to the ground, where the large ball of sponge breaks his fall, much to the chagrin of several teenagers rooting for him to miss.

Later that afternoon, I go for a walk, ostensibly to pick up some steak for dinner, but in reality to get out and enjoy the sun-shine. The daffodils are in full bloom, their heads like a parade of brilliant wimples that nuns used to wear, only yellow, much smaller, and non-denominational. A young man walks by in a junior as-sistant retailer's suit. I can tell from his haircut that he has taken advantage of the mild weather to drink a few dozen pints and howl at the moon with friends. Several slashes have been razored into the side of his head, exposing the pale white flesh beneath. The rest of his coif has been carefully arranged by a weed-whacker. The look on his face reflects, no doubt, the unqualified support he received when his boss got an eyeball-full this morning. Well, no matter. His shift is over, and by the length of his stride, I'd say he was on his way to a marathon drinking session at the Angel with his mates.

There's something odd about the piss-up. British society is rife with checks and balances, mostly enforced through shame or bylaw. Sneak into line and someone will tell you to go to the back. Forget to pay your TV tax and the lads will come around and haul it away by the rabbit ears. Park your car in the wrong spot and they will gleefully clamp and tow. Yet there is one notable exception. It is perfectly acceptable to get drunk in public and puke, urinate, or drop your trousers. There's no shame involved the next morning when you sober up. In fact, there is a new tradition of going away for a weekend *en masse* with your friends for the stag or stagette, the primary purpose of which seems to be to see how obnoxiously drunk you can get in public. This habit simply doesn't exist in North America or continental Europe. A Frenchman or Italian would be mortified if they ever got so drunk that they vomited in the streets.

I ask Mr. Trowbridge for his opinion. "I blame CAMRA," he says, as he wraps up my steaks. "When I was a lad, everyone drank Watney's Red Barrel, which had an alcohol level of around 2 per cent. You could drink ten pints of the stuff and there was no damage. Then the Campaign for Real Ale came along and the brewers saw a marketing opportunity." Low-alcohol beer was tossed in favour of hairy, 6-per-cent ale. "Now when somebody drinks ten pints, they get completely legless."

By the time I pass the Angel on the way back, the patio is full. Razor Hair is sitting at a picnic table with several of the lads from Andy's boatyard. Judging by the rate of consumption, they seem to be having a contest to see who can drink an entire keg the fastest. One good thing about having a patio jutting over the Thames; it's easy to hose down. Farther along the river, I spot Teddy and Peter at the Anchor pub. They are sitting by the front windows, which have been thrown wide open. "How did the march go?" I ask.

Teddy is into his fourth brandy at this point. "Brilliant," he says.

"A bloody disaster," says Peter, who is not far behind in the liquid refreshments category. "Nothing but country bumpkins all over the place."

Sensing that they are experts on the subject, I ask their opinion about what should be done about youths getting drunk in public. "Cane the little bastahds," offers Peter. I leave them to their musings and head home.

The barbecued steaks are delicious, and afterward, Linda and I sit out on our balcony and watch the sun set, the last rays turning the chestnut trees on the far shore to a brilliant emerald gold. Darkness slowly settles, and the lights of the town reflect off the water. We consume a bottle of Cabernet Sauvignon, then another, basking in the peace and serenity and solving the world's problems.

It is late when we finally head up to bed. I am in the bathroom brushing my teeth when Linda appears at the door. "Come quick. Somebody's stealing a boat."

I rush to the bedroom window and peer through the curtains. Sure enough, just below us, three furtive figures are hunched over one of Andy's launches. I can't make out much in the gloom, but I can hear the chain holding the boat to the dock being thrown clear. A cigarette lighter flares near the battery, then the diesel coughs into life. The boat is pushed into the main channel, and the three thieves head downstream.

I grab the bedroom phone and dial Derek. It rings for several times before there is a groggy response. "Hello?"

"Derek, it's Gord. Sorry to wake you up this late, but somebody just stole one of your boats."

Derek is suddenly alert. "Who?"

"I couldn't see, but it looked like three kids." I go to the window and peer out. The boat is doing doughnuts in the water adjacent to the Angel pub's patio. "I think they're heading toward Hambleden."

"I'll call the police."

A few minutes later a police cruiser pulls up. I watch from our bedroom window as the officers inspect the boats. Suddenly, one waves his arm and points downstream. I follow their gaze and am amazed to see the boat returning. One officer quickly pulls the cruiser out of sight and then they take cover. I get dressed and dash out the door.

I reach the corner of Station Road just as the boat approaches the dock; one of the felons leaps off with the towrope, right into the arms of a waiting policeman.

"You're under arrest!" the Bobby says.

"I didn't do anything!"

"Sure, and this is your boat too, I imagine."

"I work here!"

"What, at midnight? Come on."

Derek shows up in his four-by-four just as the police are loading the thieves into the back of their car. "We got your lads."

"Great!" Derek leans over and peers into the back of the cruiser. "Ronnie! What are you doing here?"

Ronnie is looking very sheepish. "Me and the lads came down for a ride."

It takes a great deal of arm-waving, but Derek finally convinces the police to let Ronnie and the others free. The trio are extremely grateful—not least, I suspect, because last call hasn't sounded at the Angel yet.

Every place in the world has a special smell all its own. Some cities have a unique aroma that can only be perceived first thing in the morning, when the night's air has washed away all the effluvia of the day and left only the essence of the place to pull into your lungs. Walk the streets of Paris at 5 AM, for instance, and all you can smell is the sweet, yeasty aroma of bread wafting from the bakeries on every corner. Barcelona at dawn is a magical mix of bougainvillea and diesel, and Manly Beach in Sydney smells of the sea and Norfolk pines.

It is only a month to summer solstice, and the sun comes up just after 5 AM in Henley. I arise and slip from bed, careful not to wake Linda. I put on my sneakers and exit the front door, wandering down Station Road to the river. Even the swans are asleep at this hour of the morning, squatting on the cement launch of Andy's marina, their long thick necks curled to tuck their heads beneath a wing.

I walk south along the river towpath until I am clear of the town. There has been a boozer in Mill Meadows the night before; the healthy selection of beer cans and food wrappers that litters the ground is covered with a sparkling layer of dew. I stop along the path and gaze east, where the sun is just rising over the hills on the opposite shore. The rays of light glint between the trees that top the ridge like silken hair in a comb. A breeze begins to stir, carrying the cool air trapped among the chestnut and pine. I am enveloped in the smell of forests and dawn, rich, full, earthy, and ancient. It is a smell that has existed for thousands of years, and I can easily imagine prehistoric dwellers, clad in animal skins and paddling up the river in dugout canoes, breathing in this same rich ether.

Which may explain why I am not in the least surprised to see a Roman guard setting up an army camp in front of the River & Rowing Museum. Their camp comprises two tents stitched together from an odorous collection of goatskins, and a life-sized plastic horse. The guard consists of a dozen or so men dressed in tunics, sandals, and carrying short swords. They are huddled around an iron pot on a tripod cooking a pork and bean stew over a bed of charcoal.

Even though we are talking about twelve armed men doing something extremely eccentric when most people are still in bed, there is something approachable about a soldier in a miniskirt. I introduce myself to the bean stirrer. Marcus is a photocopy repairman in his early thirties and a cohort of the Ermine Street Guard, a Roman military reconstruction society invited to Henley by the museum as part of this month's exhibition on Roman inhabitation along the Thames. "What's the most enjoyable part of your hobby?" I ask.

"I have a full-scale catapult," replies Marcus. "I take it to castles and fire melons at the walls."

There's a lot to be said for tossed fruit salad. "Any downside?"

"Wearing a skirt," says Marcus. "It's nippy."

Marcus also has a nasty, pointy spear and a large shield made of authentic plywood. "Do you do battle re-enactments?" I ask.

"No, but the BBC does hire us now and again for historical documentaries. I got to whip Boudicca personally."

We are interrupted by what the Brits call *the weather*. One of the most frustrating aspects of living in a river town like Henley is that you are at the bottom of a valley, and thus have a restricted view. For an optimist like myself, this means that if the skies are sunny, then they may very well be clear all the way to France. On the other hand, if it is grey and overcast, there might be a cheerful patch of blue lurking right behind yonder hill.

The downside, of course, is that things tend to sneak up on you. I notice that it has suddenly grown very dark indeed. Glancing up, I catch sight of a particularly malevolent cloud bearing directly down upon our general location, accompanied by a white curtain of hail undulating below. Everyone dashes for cover beneath the entrance to the River & Rowing Museum. A slushy mix of ice and rain pounds down upon the river. At the height of its fury, the storm rips huge branches from the trees on the far shore and pummels the boats moored along the banks. It is a crescendo of wind and ice beating everything in its path into the ground.

And, just as suddenly, it is over. The storm moves eastward, leaving piles of ice steaming on the ground. A pack of rowers in brightly coloured plastic kayaks appear in midstream, their double oars flashing and sparkling. A rainbow, stretching a full 180 degrees across the sky, glows warmly against the rapidly retreating black cloud. Within a few minutes, nothing of its passage remains, except for a pile of wet beans where the pot has overturned onto the ground. Marcus cheerfully scoops the mess up and plops it back into the pot, carefully picking out errant bits of grass and twigs.

"You're not going to *eat* that lot, are you?"

"Of course not," says Marcus. "We'll feed it to the tourists."

I return to Boathouse Reach to discover Linda and I have a busy day ahead. Linda's job has been going very well—so well, in fact, that she suspects her consulting skills may no longer be required when she reaches the end of her year-long contract. Holidays and weekends are thus focused on seeing as much of the countryside as possible.

First on the list is lunch in the Chilterns. We drive westwards from Henley, past Rotherfield Peppard, then turn southwest toward Cane End. Halfway along Horsepond Road, we come to The Reformation pub in Gallowstree Common. A sandwich board by the road boasts full roast lunch of beef or turkey, with all the trimmings. A century ago, all you'd have to do was throw in a hanging and the Sunday afternoon would be complete.

The Reformation is a two-storey structure painted white with black trim. The architecture is mid–nineteenth century, and it appears to have been originally built as a mill and bakery. Tables are scattered around the front yard in haphazard fashion. The pub has a rambling, improvised nature that invites you to come in and feel at home. We enter through the main door and turn left. A large conservatory, built on one side of the pub, has been declared non-smoking. It is largely empty, so we pick a table in the sunshine and sit down.

Almost immediately, a short, dark-haired man rushes in. "No, no, you cannot sit there!" Viktor has a thick Russian accent and a theatrical impression of his own importance. We gather up our coats and he bustles us off to a tiny room adjacent to the kitchen entrance. It is decorated with a large log fireplace, a painting of rustic peasants getting drunk at a wedding, and two golden Lab puppies snuffling about making friends with everyone.

We go to the bar and order two turkey plates and some Brakspear beer. They have brewed a new ale for the autumn, Falling Leaf, which is light and golden. While we are waiting for George the publican to pour our pints, an older man enters. He is dressed in tweed and has a long, thin neck to match his nose. He studies the menu board, which states that the roasts of the day are beef and turkey. He turns to the publican and speaks with a very plummy accent. "Tell me my good man, what are your mains today?"

George glances briefly at the board, just to make sure some-one hasn't erased the six-inch letters. "Roast beef and roast turkey."

The man, who has cupped one hand behind his ear to aid his hearing, looks genuinely puzzled. "Extraordinary! Did you say roast *toucan*?"

"Yeah. Next week we're doing duck-billed platypus with gravy and mash."

"In that case, I shall have the beef."

"You got it, Guv."

We return to our table, where Viktor shortly appears with a bowl of horseradish. "You'll love this with your beef," he announces.

"We ordered turkey," notes Linda.

"Oh, a thousand pardons." Viktor rushes back into the kitchen with a look of murder on his face. He shortly appears with a bowl of cranberry sauce and our meals.

There is something unique about sitting at an English country pub with a pint of real ale and a Sunday roast. The turkey breast is moist and tender, the potatoes roasted to perfection, the gravy smooth and silky. Even the stuffing, a mix of sage, onion, and sausage, is delicious. We order another round of Falling Leaf and sit back in our chairs. I can't help but notice that the non-smoking section is virtually deserted, but hey, Viktor is having one of those days. He enters stage left from the kitchen with two dessert cakes and tries to serve them to the only couple in the section. "We didn't order those."

"I'm terribly sorry." Viktor flings open the door to the kitchen. "Number 8 didn't order these!"

The cook shouts back. "That's for number 16."

Viktor looks over his shoulder. "But they haven't even had their main plates cleaned off!" He storms into the kitchen and there is a resounding crash as two slices of cake are flung across the room. The door swings open, and Viktor reappears, all sweetness and light. "How was the meal?"

"Fantastic!" says Linda.

"Tremendous!" I agree.

"Good. Would you like some coffee or dessert?"

"No, that was very filling," says Linda. "Not a smidgen of room left!"

Viktor bows and backs away. We take the opportunity to guzzle down our beers, throw down some money, and bolt for the door. I just hope we left enough tip to keep him from chasing us down Horsepond Road with a cleaver.

Our final stop that afternoon is the Acton Annual Art Show. On the whole, I find local art exhibitions fascinating. Why pander to artistic norms when you can go bounding off in flights of fancy that would make Picasso weep in envy? We recently wandered into a showing of watercolours in the Henley Exhibition and Trade Centre where a sign said the Shiplake Art Collective was mounting its annual show. I was astounded by the sophisticated manner in which the various artists on display had managed to distort perspective on seemingly innocuous landscapes in a manner that engendered not only amazement, but epilepsy, if you stared at them too long.

Imagine then, my disappointment when we arrived at Barn Gallery in Acton and are confronted by the works of some seriously talented people. The gallery is situated in an undulating landscape, the verdant fields rolling gently off into the distant Thames Valley. The farm itself consists of a series of outbuildings that form a protective courtyard, their rough stone and brick walls supporting a long line of red shale tiles. Scattered throughout the paddocks are a score of sculptures in wood and steel and stone, each one framed by a backdrop of thick green grass or a duck pond.

My eye is immediately drawn to a series of willowy, seven-foot, copper pitchforks, the tines encasing a blue glass orb. The artist has entitled the work *The Eyes of Mesmer*, which is apt. Linda is captivated by a series of stainless steel calla lilies, sculpted so finely that they seem to be swaying in the gentle breeze. Works that are more sensitive to the elements—oil landscapes, jewellery, and glasswork—are on display in the largest barn. I am especially fond of the work of a glassblower based in the Cotswolds. Strings of tiny glass birds in flight have been woven into a loose mesh of glass cloth, which has then been moulded into platters and bowls. I'm sure that an elf would feel quite at home eating his breakfast cereal out of one.

We are about to exit when we pass a side gallery dedicated to the annual competition. One particular piece catches my eye, a vivid abstract landscape of the countryside, a wide valley flanked by gently rolling, tree-covered hills. Above it, in a manner reminiscent of Gauguin, float a man and a woman upon an azure sky, gazing into one another's fishy eyes with obvious rapture. A gold ribbon hangs off the right corner.

I turn to find Alan peering eagerly over my shoulder. "Do you like it?"

"It's amazing."

Alan's face is gripped by uncertainty. "You're just saying that to please me."

"You're right. It's rubbish."

A smile breaks out on Alan's face. "Brilliant."

If there's one thing I admire about the British, it's their ability to take a compliment.

11

JUNE

Come Together

No doubt about it, the English are *definitely* odd. Exhibit A is the Come Together Experience, an outdoor fair that has sprouted in Mill Meadows overnight like a crop of magic mushrooms. When we arrive mid-afternoon, half a dozen brightly coloured tents are simultaneously hosting various musicians. We sprint past the bandstand in which ten people are participating in a drum workshop sponsored by the mental health association, and stop to admire a punk sax quartet performing their latest hit, "Sexy Teenage Bitch Goddess." A small girl in an angel costume and her puppy dance to the tune, enraptured.

It is the June first weekend, and half the town is out to celebrate the warm summer weather. We gravitate to a row of stalls featuring a large selection of stoner gear. A young man in camouflage jams is selling pixie caps made from brown and green felt to anyone looking for that just-been-thumped-with-a-cricket-bat look. Farther down, a woman in purple cornrows is retailing dildos made from black balsam wood. I buy one for Grandmother's mantelpiece.

We bump into a juggler using oversized chopsticks to twirl his nobbin, a two-foot dowel with felt-covered weights on the ends. I have never understood the entertainment value here; in my opinion, it would be a far more enjoyable spectacle if he simply shampooed his hair with honey and then whacked at bees when they landed on his head. Now, that I would pay to see.

As odd as the English are, they just don't hold a candle to the French. Just as we are leaving, we bump into Felix. I don't recognize him without his tall white chef's hat and apron until he grabs me by the shoulders and plants a big kiss on my cheek. "You come to my barbecue!" he announces.

"When?"

"Now!"

"Where?"

Felix points to an unoccupied picnic table. "Grab one end and follow me!"

We make a hasty exit from the park. Fortunately, we don't have far to go, but my arms are at least two inches longer by the time we reach the chef's home. Felix and his wife Rose live in an apartment above the Packrat Antique Shoppe on Friday Street. The back door of the apartment opens up onto a tiny garden that is completely enclosed by a high brick wall, a handy thing considering how much of the yard furniture belongs to Henley Council. In addition to the picnic table, Felix has scrounged up some umbrellas that curiously match those normally seen in front of the ice cream stand in Mill Meadows. The barbecue itself is a tiny charcoal model of the type normally featured in a coroner's fire reconstruction. Felix grabs a hair dryer and points it under the coals, sending up a torrent of sparks.

"Go to the kitchen and fetch the food!" he commands. I wonder if an extinguisher wouldn't be a better idea.

Inside, Rose is busily frying up some homemade egg rolls as appetizers. A huge plate of marinated shish kebabs sits to one side: bamboo splints of chicken, beef, and spicy sausage. Beside the platter is a smaller plate of mysterious dark meat. "What's that?" I ask.

"Heart and liver," she explains. "Very good!"

My follow-up question—"Heart and liver of *what*?"—dies on my lips.

Felix's guests soon arrive: Ian and Leslie, and Oliver and his wife, Jo. Oliver and Ian congregate beside the barbeque and talk tennis.

"Going to Wimbledon this year?" says Oliver.

"No, didn't get tickets," replies Ian.

"Just as well, spares you the sight of Henman going out in the second round."

"Why do you root for him then?" I ask.

"Because the British love a loser," says Oliver.

The sun beats down and the wine flows. After my third glass of red, I am feeling a bit peckish, and when Felix offers me a skewer of roast heart, I am more than happy to gobble it down, pronouncing it perfectly delicious. By the time late evening rolls around, Linda and I have had enough salad and offal. We bid everyone adieu and head for home.

We are still more than a hundred yards from Boathouse Reach when we hear the party. Adrian, a young man in his twenties who lives in the townhouse a few doors down, is holding a fancy-dress fete to celebrate—as far as I can tell—the invention of the amplifier. A largish group of friends dressed as rhinestone cowboys strut around the marina in white leisure suits and leopard skin Stetsons, barfing up lager, throwing chicken bones at the swans, and generally behaving like prats. Adrian invites us to join in, but we politely decline.

Around 1 AM, I am roused from bed by someone banging at our portal. I open the front door to discover a man in a blue sequin strapless dress holding a can of cider in each hand and teetering on six-inch heels. When he realizes his mistake, he asks where Adrian lives. I point in the direction of the nearest sewer grate and turn off the porch light.

Sunday morning we arise late, and I set off to pick up a carton of eggs for brunch. Even though it is past noon, Adrian's house is as quiet as a sepulchre. I walk around to the marina out front, where Derek is taking advantage of a lull in boat rentals to have a coffee. I am surprised to note that the marina is clean. "What happened to all the chicken bones?"

"I threw them back onto Adrian's balcony."

A sudden thought strikes me. "Does *The New Orleans* have a sound system?"

"A real beauty. Why?"

"I think a little music might be nice. You know, something that Adrian and his friends might appreciate."

Derek gives a wicked grin. "I'll check what's available."

I purchase my carton of eggs at Waitrose and head back along New Street. Just as I turn onto the riverfront, I spot a man with a shirt tagged *Dave* rounding up members of the juvenile swan gang I had nicknamed the Craps. Four swans squat on the ground, their legs bound by Velcro strips. They look as though they're on their way to be guests of honour at a roast. I stop to find out what's going on, and, hopefully, cadge an invitation.

As it turns out, Dave is not a sous chef, but a bird herder. The swans are being uprooted in advance of the Henley Regatta. In order to protect them from the inevitable influx of boats, about 150 swans are annually taken to a sanctuary pond near Egham where they are kept until the hubbub dies down.

I love the way the English treat our feathered little friends. Just to place it all in context, the government recently failed to pass a specific law making it illegal to spit on train employees, but here's what it says in my egg carton:

> Our straw bedded eggs are laid by hens housed in barns, in which there is plenty of space to roam and run around. Hens enjoy scratching, preening and dust-bathing and the deep straw covered floor encourages these social activities. The

hens have easy access to clean food and water at all times and nest boxes provide a safe private place in which to lay their eggs. This makes for contented hens and tasty eggs!

I'm not sure how they know the hens are happy—perhaps they have a psychologist analyzing their fowl thoughts.

At any rate, one can ensure the blissfulness of one's pet, including chickens, by taking it to church and having it blessed. I know this because, as I continue on my way home, I spot a posting on the bulletin board beside the entrance to St. Mary's Church inviting parishioners to bring their pets in for special ministration. I contemplate having my eggs blessed, but I suspect I might be a tad premature. A signboard on the sidewalk has an equally alluring invitation: "Visit the top of the tower, only £2." If there's anything I enjoy, it's sitting up high with a carton of eggs and peering down into people's backyards.

Just inside the main doors, a retired kindergarten teacher in a fluffy brown cardigan is seated in front of a small desk with a cash box and an SAS walkie-talkie. I pay my entrance fee and she hands me an illustrated guide. She pushes a button on the walkie-talkie and lets Alec know I'm on my way up. She then tells me to watch my step and not to run with scissors.

She didn't mention not to read the pamphlet as I ascend, however. The illustrated guide notes that the tower was built by rich local landowners in 1390, just after the Black Death. Nothing like a plague to whet the appetite for religious donations, is there?

Halfway up, I come to the ringing chamber. It is roughly twelve feet across, with a series of white ropes dangling from the ceiling. One side of the room is occupied by a large wooden cabinet that holds the workings for the tower clock. Installed in 1877 by J.W. Benson of Ludgate Hill, London, the top of the mechanical device is visible through a glass window. A flywheel connected to a series of arms begins to rotate and the quarter-hour is automatically chimed.

I ascend to the bell chamber immediately above. The white ropes from the room below are connected to a series of brass bells. There are nine in total, the largest being just over a metre in diameter and weighing one tonne. They sit in wooden cradles, and when the ropes are pulled, they rock back and forth, their clappers striking the single note.

I finally emerge at the top of the tower. It is square, perhaps four and a half metres on a side, and surrounded by a low, crenellated wall. Thick copper lightning strips, covered in a patina of green oxide, run down from the apex to the ground. Pigeon guano, some of it an inch thick, has collected beneath their nocturnal roost.

"It's an amazing view, isn't it?" Alec, a slightly built man with a walkie-talkie on a strap around his neck, is standing beside the entranceway. By the way he is clutching a book of saints to his breast, I get the impression he's a tad nervous of heights. Regardless, Alec is correct about the view. To the north and south, the Thames stretches in a gentle curve of blue. To the east, Henley Bridge bustles with traffic and, to the west, Market Place and Hart Street are filled with pedestrians. I am struck by myriad gardens that wend their way back from the main streets into the bowels of the residential blocks. Each plot is concealed from its neighbour by a high wall and thick vines, but there are no barriers to scrutiny from the high tower. I am somewhat disappointed to discover that it is a bit too high to make out what exactly is flapping in the breeze from the various clotheslines in view, but I hesitate to ask Alec if he might be packing binoculars, feeling fairly certain that anyone who reads hagiographies as a pastime probably knows a pervert when he sees one.

Alec pries himself away from the railing long enough to approach. "Is there anything you'd like to know about the tower?"

"Has anyone ever thrown themselves off?"

Apparently, this is not a good question. Alec turns a pale shade of green and rushes back to the entranceway where he has stashed a Thermos and takes a healthy nip. From the way the colour returns to his cheeks, I get the impression he is packing a hefty tot of rum. At any rate, he glances nervously sideways toward the edge of the tower while forming a reply. "Not that I know."

"I hope you don't mind me asking, but why does someone with an aversion to heights volunteer for tower duty?"

Alec smiles wanly. "I feel I'm a little closer to the Lord."

One more swig, I suspect, and he'll be a lot higher than the tower. I bid Alec a pleasant afternoon and head back down, idly wondering if the Reverend also blesses cuckoos.

By the time I reach home, Derek has located a CD of a Dixieland band and has *The New Orleans*'s loudspeakers cranked right up. One can only hope that Adrian appreciates a banjo quartet at two hundred watts as much as I do.

I am walking past Latrino's on Hart Street a few days later when I notice an intriguing poster. Apparently, the nightclub is promoting the *All New Gentlemen's Night*, featuring table dancing where *Beautiful Exotic Dancers Perform Live on Stage and Personal Private Dances For You!* In the poster, a man in a top hat and white gloves is lighting a cigar using a £20 note while two blonde women in black bikinis finger the straps of their thongs. I note, with some dismay, that the date for the special engagement was the previous evening.

It suddenly occurs to me that there are no pornography shops in Henley. They're all the rage in London, of course. I once came across an S&M shop in Soho where the window display featured a mannequin dressed up in a black leather mask and a panty and bra set made of red leather vinyl with twin spikes sticking out at the nipples. In fact, I still have it. But there is nothing even remotely similar to be seen in Henley; the most pornographic video for rent at Blockbuster is one of those 1970s epics where the plumbing lad spends his day servicing horny vicars' wives with a resigned leer. Most of the newsagent's do carry a selection of lad's magazines wrapped in plastic and piled on the top shelf, well out of most people's reach and line of sight. One would have to be either very pious, going about all day peering heavenward, to spot these pneumatic angels perched on high, or very tall.

My general impression is that the good people of Henley are seriously under-indulged, so I suspect that the *All New Gentlemen's Night* must have been a resounding success. When I return home, I spot Owen and stop to ask if he happened to attend. "No way. They wanted eight quid to get in."

"That's not overly expensive, is it?"

"Are you kiddin'? That's four pints, *innit*? Besides, you got more important things to worry about here, mate." He points to a rash of tiny black spots all over my dahlias. Leaning over for a better look, I am horrified to discover a horde of tiny bugs crawling over the stalks.

"What the hell is this?" I ask.

"Them's aphids, my lad. Nasty little buggers, they is."

I do a little research and learn that the aphid is capable of stunting plant growth, transmitting viruses, and even committing credit-card fraud. Curiously, these nasty little suckers are carried by ants from plant to plant, where they set up little dairy farms, milking the aphids of the sweet honeydew that excrete from their udders. I have a sudden vision of a group of ants sitting around a Thermos of tea at break time reading their version of the *Sun* tabloid. "Topless Aphids! Pix inside!"

Taking my trusty squeeze bottle of Fairy Liquid dish soap, I give the dairy farm a healthy squirt of suds, washing the perverted little blighters into insect oblivion. *Aah*, the joys of gardening.

My ministrations are interrupted by the phone. When I answer, I am greeted by an accent that is a mix of English public school and Irish brogue. "Gohdun! How are you?"

I recognize the voice of Simon de Normann, a publisher based in Henley. I had sent some sample chapters of my diary to his office to see if he had any interest in publishing my work. "What's up?"

"I like your Henley project and I'm interested in talking to you about it. Are you busy this morning?"

I glance back through the open door toward the dahlias. "Well, I had a few important engagements, but I think I can brush them off."

"Excellent. Shall we say an hour then?"

I dress up in what I consider to be writerly attire: a black turtleneck sweater and tweed jacket. I pack my book outline into a satchel and set off for Simon's home and office, located in a cul-de-sac several hundred feet north of Boathouse Reach.

Simon's house, like all the others along the road, is a three-storey nineteenth-century monstrosity of red brick and carved sandstone. The lintel stone above the front door features a troll drooling over a rather well-endowed nymph. The tableau is complemented by the doorbell, a wrought-iron depiction of a monk hiking his robe to take a leak. I pull on his knob and ring the bell.

Nobody answers. I glance at my watch, and it is indeed the appointed hour. I wait several more minutes then lean over and glance through the mail slot. All I can see is a bit of rug-covered foyer and a set of stairs leading to the second floor. Feeling a bit foolish, I straighten up and glance about, hoping that no one saw my snooping. I am just about ready to leave, when Simon clambers down the set of stairs and opens the door.

The publisher possesses a mop of straight brown hair and a round face. He is short, and his shoulders are stooped. "You *must* excuse me, I have someone on the phone. Come on up."

Inside, the hallway wallpaper is peeling off in huge chunks, and the handrail is a litigation lawyer's dream. The smell emanating from the carpet reminds me of an incontinent basset hound.

Simon's office faces out over the road. Once upon a time, it was a rather grand drawing room, with a twelve-foot ceiling, immense bay window, and large fireplace, but the effect has been marred with a plethora of modern laminate furniture, the kind you buy in a box and assemble with a tiny wrench. A half-dozen or so paperback books, the entire backlist of de Normann Press, occupy one corner of a bookshelf.

Simon resumes his conversation on the phone, and I am left to peruse the office and try not to listen. A nineteenth-century portrait of a rather effete-looking man is mounted above the fireplace. He is wearing white breeches and a red military jacket with brass buttons. In the background is a battlefield littered with crushed cannon and the corpses of British cavalrymen. His right arm is raised, the white-gloved hand open, as though inviting the viewer to gaze upon his achievement with awe.

Simon puts his hand over the mouthpiece for a moment. "The Crimean War."

"What?"

Simon nods toward the painting. "You know, the Charge of the Light Brigade."

Ah. Nothing like a senseless massacre to cheer up a room, I always say. "So, who's Wonder Boy?"

Simon hangs up the phone. "*Lord* Lucan, of course. He led the brigade. I'm a cousin of the current Lord, you know."

"Is that the same Lord Lucan who disappeared?" I am referring, of course, to the upper-class twit who crept into his London home late one dark night in 1974 and inadvertently beat the nanny to death, thinking it was his estranged wife.

"The very same." Simon shakes his head. "A strange and sad situation, that. For years after he disappeared, there were reported sightings around the world, but he's never been found."

"What do you think happened to him?"

Simon glances left and right then lowers his voice. "I have an acquaintance who was a colonel in the SAS. He saw the FBI file. In essence, it said, don't bother looking for him."

Simon gives me a knowing look, but I have no idea what he means. Does he mean that somebody stuffed him into a wood-chipper, he's had an operation that changed him into a Peruvian llama, or what? You've got to be careful about how you phrase questions like that. Instead, I go over my idea for a year in Henley.

Simon listens attentively then leans back and thoughtfully stares at the ceiling. "It's all very good, but I think you should spice it up a bit."

"What do you mean?"

"Henley is quite the hotspot, you know."

I glance out the window. "I hadn't really noticed."

"Oh, there's all kinds of things going on: corrupt politicians, adulterous wives, oodles of naughtiness."

"Sorry, I don't have the slightest clue when it comes to that sort of thing."

"Not to worry, I'll handle all that." The phone rings and Simon picks it up. He waves in dismissal, and I find my own way out.

Summer solstice arrives, and the usual tribe of loonies invade Stonehenge to party and riot. Since I don't particularly like to mix the two, I decide it is time to check out Henley's local Stone Age site instead.

Of course, Druid's Temple, on Wargrave Road, is neither. It dates back around forty-five hundred years ago, long before druids ever donned capes and lurked about. It is probably a pre-Celtic burial chamber, originally sited on the isle of Jersey. How it got from Jersey to Henley is a fascinating story in itself.

I was mooching around the gift shop of the River & Rowing Museum when I came across a slim book entitled, *General Henry Conway and His Great Temple*. It was written by local historian Brian Read, and tells the tale of one of the most eccentric individuals ever to live in Henley, which is saying a lot.

Born in 1721, Conway distinguished himself as a parliamentarian, military officer, and gentleman farmer. In a portrait by Thomas Gainsborough, he is wearing a military uniform and wig and gazing in a benevolent manner into the far distance. He was, in the words of his cousin, Horace Walpole (an accomplished diarist and butt-kisser), noted for his "kindness, generous charity, and graceful eloquence."

His home, Park Place, was a large estate covering approximately 1.5 square kilometres on the eastern shore of the Thames, just across from Henley. After buying Park Place from Frederick, Prince of Wales (and father of George III), Conway set about modelling it after his own tastes. Conway built a Greek amphitheatre, a lavender distillery, several thousand metres of secret tunnels, and a stone archway known as Conway's Bridge. The bridge is still in use by all traffic passing between Henley and Wargrave.

Back in 1778, when General Conway was governor of Jersey, the French declared war on Britain and promptly attempted to reclaim the Channel Islands. Conway, foreseeing hostilities, had invested time and effort in reinforcing the main town of St. Helier, and the islanders were able to repulse numerous invasions. As a show of gratitude, they commissioned his portrait by Gainsborough and deeded the temple to the governor as a gift.

Rather than being miffed at getting 140 tonnes of ancient rock, Conway was delighted. In 1788, he arranged to transport the pile of granite to Tower Wharf in London and then barge it up the Thames to Park Place. He situated it on a prominent hill overlooking the valley where, in Walpole's words, "it looks very high-priestly. It is impossible not to be pleased with so very rare an antiquity."

I ride my bike south along Wargrave Road to Conway's Bridge. It is a graceful arch, perhaps fifteen metres in length, built from roughly hewn stone scavenged from Reading Abbey. The entrance to the road leading up to the Druid Temple is located some 140 metres from the bridge. I ride my bike south along Wargrave Road until I come to an estate entrance. There is a small, unoccupied gatehouse to one side and a large sign that says *Private Road—no entrance*. The wooden gate is open, however, so they can't be that worried about illiterate intruders, can they? I decide that, if I'm nicked, I shall plead dyslexia.

The paved driveway that winds its way steeply up the hill has a somewhat neglected look; perhaps it's the potholes full of Foster's lager cans. When I reach the top of the hill, I stop to admire the house at the end of the drive. It is a genuine Frank Lloyd Wright home, a long, sinuous arm of honey-coloured stone curling out from the side of the hill, designed in the 1950s by the famous American architect. Curtains have been drawn across the large windows that look over the valley, and it has the silent air about it that clings to unoccupied homes.

I spot my quarry. The temple consists of about two dozen stones approximately 1.5 metres tall and one metre across. They have been arranged in a circle roughly six metres in diameter in the middle of a large, manicured lawn. I park my bike and walk across the grass toward the monument. The stones are made of pink granite and coated with a thick patina of white and grey lichen. Inside the temple, five cap rocks have been positioned, recreating the cells found by the original excavators. None of the rocks bear any ancient writings, but a modern plaque has been mounted on the entrance wall, bearing an inscription in appropriately purple prose: "Hidden for centuries from the gaze of mortal man, this ancient monument, these stones, these altars where human blood offered in sacrifice flowed for imagined gods."

I conjure up the image of a bloodthirsty high priest pulling the heart out of some victim's beating breast, perhaps a Waitrose clerk, but, frankly, it's a stretch. The temple is bereft of the quiet, brooding majesty that accompanies Stonehenge. Somehow, the knowledge that it has been moved from its original place has completely dissipated the dark, cryptic magic you feel when standing among the ancient stones of a lost civilization.

The arrival of the groundskeeper and his guard dog interrupts my search for pre-Celtic vibes. He is a small, nearsighted man and his springer spaniel looks thoroughly capable of licking someone to death. He is very cross, perhaps because I am standing in his flowerbed. "This is private property," he announces in a thick Greek accent. "You must leave!"

I hold up my camera. "I just came up to have a look at the temple and take a few pictures."

"No pictures!" He pulls out his cellphone and waves it in my face. "Forbidden!"

A cellphone isn't exactly as menacing as a pitchfork, but I read somewhere you can get a nasty brain tumour if you hold one too close, so I back away a few steps and stumble over his dog, which yelps.

"You go now!"

I resist the temptation to take his picture. Getting on my bike, I console myself with the thought of the Elgin marbles, sitting in the British Museum thousands of kilometres from their home. I wish the little Greek gardener a nice day.

It is a fine, sunny morning, and I am contemplating the best way to waste it when I receive a call. "Gohdun!"

"Simon?"

"Can you come for coffee later this morning?" It turns out Simon is meeting with an old friend at the moment, consoling her over a recent divorce. As soon as she is gone, however, he promises we can talk about my work. I agree to meet him at 11 AM

I arrive at the coffee shop at the appointed hour and join Simon at a sidewalk table. A pale blue Mercedes sedan pulls up, and his friend emerges. Amanda is in her early fifties, a thin, stylish woman with short, ash-blonde hair and a smile that appears to be continuously on the verge of tears. I sit and chat amiably with them for about an hour, tactfully trying to avoid any phrase that includes irreconcilable differences, two-faced bastard, and mistress. At noon, Simon calls for the bill and announces to the air, "Well, that was nice; perhaps we should move along to Loch Fyne Restaurant?"

Amanda follows us down the street, and now that the ice has been broken with an invitation to dine, feels free to regale me with the fact, thank God, that she's found the most wonderful new lover to make her forget her husband. I wait in vain for Simon to intervene, but he is the epitome of what the English like to call discretion, and everyone else calls spineless. I thus find myself sitting at an outdoor table in Market Place gravely nodding through the sordid details of her former husband's mid-life crisis with a Belgian tart. Since by now the three litres of tea have distended my bladder to the point where it is interfering with breathing, I excuse myself and head for the loo. When I return, I find that, as if by magic, the publisher has disappeared. "Where did Simon go?"

Amanda waves a hand off into the distance. "Oh, he's gone off to the office to sort out some business."

I suddenly get the odd feeling that I'm being set up. I dig out my cellphone and call Simon. "What's going on here?"

"Remember how you were saying that you needed some spice in your book? Sleazy politicians and adulteresses and such?"

"I did?"

Simon lowers his voice to a whisper. "You know what happened during the election?"

I assume he is referring to Gyles Groodey. "Yeah, so what?"

Simon's voice takes on a hiss. "You're sitting beside *the other woman*."

Suddenly, it all makes sense. I turn and smile mildly in Amanda's direction, all the while trying to keep my voice under control. "And what do you expect *me* to do about it?"

"You're the journalist. Order a few bottles of wine and write down whatever she says."

I quietly curse his mother and hang up. "I'm sorry, but I have to leave," I announce.

"It's me, isn't it?" Tears begin to run down Amanda's cheeks.

"No, it's just that I'm not eating lunch this week. I'm on a diet, you see."

"What kind of diet?"

"Uh, the All-You-Can-Eat-Just-Not-at-Lunch Diet."

"I've never heard of that one."

"It's all the rage in France." I glance at a non-existent watch on my wrist. "Look at the time, must go."

"But, what shall I tell Simon?"

"Tell him he's a silly prat." I head off feeling like the perfect louse, even though it is Simon who needs a good boot in the arse.

The incident with Simon leaves a foul taste in my mouth for several days, and it isn't until Teddy calls and invites Linda and me to lunch at Leander that my mood finally lifts. It is raining by the time we have to leave, so we take our car.

With the Henley Regatta starting in just a few days, the grounds have now been completely cordoned off, and guards are on duty to direct huge Range Rovers pulling trailers filled with white, red, and yellow boats. Refrigerated lorries, lawn-mowing tractors, and catering trucks all scurry about the grounds on a million last-minute chores.

I drop Linda off at the entrance and try to park in the Leander lot. A young woman dressed in a bright orange tunic shakes her head. "I'm sorry sir, you can't park here. Please go out that gate and follow directions." At the gate, a bucktoothed teenager points his cigarette in the direction of Dover. I drive through several muddy fields until I finally come to rest at the base of White Hill, about two hundred metres farther from Leander than if I had walked from home. I pick my way through the muck back to the club.

Teddy and Linda are well settled in by the time I empty the mud from my shoes and join them.

"Good you could get here," says Teddy. He is a bit distracted by the imminent start of the regatta and orders me a Brakspear bitter, then proceeds to absentmindedly drink it when it arrives at our table. "Have you got your Steward's Enclosure badges yet for Saturday?"

"Yes, Teddy."

"Good. I'll get you some for Saturday then."

I am about to remind Teddy once again when our first course arrives. The soup—carrot and coriander—is hot, fresh, and delicious. The baked cod is served on a bed of mashed potatoes and spinach, with a butter and herb sauce.

"Old Davidge might not make it tomorrow; he burst a blood vessel or something and had to go to hospital," says Teddy. According to Teddy, Chris Davidge is a famous rower and one of the founders of the Barn Cottage Boat Club.

"Oh my," says Linda. "Was it serious?"

"He didn't recommend anyone else try it."

We finish our meal, and Teddy offers to drive us around to show us the grounds. Getting into his tiny Peugeot, Teddy puts the car into first and races off at five kilometres per hour. There is no room for cars behind us to pass, and when Teddy finally pulls over, a motorist races by, honking his horn. Teddy squints after the departing car. "I don't recognize him. I wonder if it's a friend?"

"Probably not, Teddy. He was waving with one finger."

We turn and head back, past at least a kilometre of white canvas marquees. We come to a point where the road is partially blocked by a septic tank truck. Teddy rolls down his window and shouts, "Come on, move!" As we ease our way past, the operator pulls a lever and I am blasted through the window by a brown cloud coming from a valve on the side of the truck. The exhaust scoots up my nose and covers my head in a fine mist of vaporized shit. Gasping and retching, I curse the day I passed on the opportunity to purchase a rocket-propelled grenade.

Teddy finally pulls over near the river. The course has been laid out in the middle of the Thames, straight and true for more than a mile. Thick white posts have been driven into the river mud, then fifteen-metre beams strung out along the length to act as a barrier to errant boats plying the length. The course is just wide enough to accommodate two boats, and there is a passing lane on each side. I can't imagine how the outside lanes are going to handle all the river traffic.

The sun comes out and falls upon the puddles of water that have accumulated from the recent shower. Steam rises lazily from the pavement, and the air immediately takes on a dampness that leaves me hot and uncomfortable in my wool jacket and pants.

Teddy, however, is oblivious to the heat. He stares out onto the course, his eyes misty with the memories of times past.

"Wait until you see the regatta," he says. "It's the most wonderful sight on earth."

12

JULY

The Regatta

The first morning of the Henley Regatta dawns cloudy, but the rain appears to be holding off. By about 10 AM, a procession of men and women begin to funnel down along the shoreline from the train station. The women are dressed in colourful summer dresses and large straw hats. The men are wearing a wide array of blazers, some in purple with pink piping, others with thick white and red stripes. The women are lugging wicker picnic baskets, and everyone is carrying an umbrella.

I dress up in my new blazer, a rather nifty affair of black Italian wool and brass buttons, and Linda dons her special summer dress, a floral pattern in silk. As we pass Andy's marina, Jack comes out and waves over one of his lads. "Take Mr. and Mrs. Cope across to the grounds." We clamber aboard one of the launches and the lad navigates us under the bridge to the dock in front of the Leander Club.

There is no sight of Teddy anywhere, so we don our pink day badges and head toward the grounds. The Competitors' Enclosure consists of about a dozen long tents, fronted by a large grassy area. The crews, dressed in a wide array of Lycra uniforms, are carrying their boats down to the shore. We scoot out of the way as eight men hustle by with a fifteen-metre torpedo of fibreglass and aluminum.

The finish line is located at the end of the competitors' area, just inside the Steward's Enclosure. A white judge's box sits on stilts in the middle of the river. As we watch, a crew of eight men in crimson and white come flashing past, and the amplified voice of the announcer echoes up and down the river: "Harvard University, of the United States of America, defeats the University of Leicester by two lengths."

A car park has been set out on the lawn behind the Steward's Enclosure. A half-dozen people drinking champagne are clustered around a butter-coloured Bentley convertible parked under the shade of a chestnut tree. I notice that several dozen cars have chairs and tables set up behind them, most protected from the elements by portable marquees. "It's like a high-end tailgate party," says Linda. "I wonder why they go to all that trouble."

We continue down to the Regatta Enclosure, which is designed for the general viewing public and competitors. Our admission badges to the upper-class Steward's Enclosure don't come into effect for another day or so; we're forced to slum with the common folk for today. About five hundred people are sitting in the grandstand, cheering on their teams. A large roar goes up as an Irish eight in blue and gold hurtles by. Even above the din of the crowd, I can hear the cox calling out the strokes: "*Hunn! Tuu! Hree! Fuuh!*" The sun pokes out from behind the clouds, and the mood of the crowd brightens. Women doff their shawls to reveal naked shoulders and skimpy summer dresses, and a long queue forms behind the ice cream cart. Crew members saunter by in club blazers of mauve and purple, pausing to greet competitors.

The Henley Regatta was first started in 1839, after the sport became popular among the young swells in London and spread to the universities of Cambridge and Oxford. Henley, which had one of the few stretches in the river that ran straight for a mile, announced that it would present a grand challenge cup and one hundred guineas to the fastest amateur team in an eight-man boat. First Trinity, Cambridge, dressed in blue striped jerseys, won the prize. The first races were run in heavy wooden skiffs, but over the years, the boats became lighter and the number of races grew. Men and women from all over the world now compete in twenty different categories over the course of the five-day event.

The list of competitors is long; today's races include some eighty elimination heats. The program lists all of the athletes by weight, in stone. I ask a woman sitting in front of me how many pounds are in a stone. "Fourteen," she replies, in that tone of voice that the English use when dealing with idiots and Yanks.

I think that Americans should come up with some weasel words just to bug British visitors to the States.

"How much is petrol in your station, my good man?"

"Two bucks a buttnuck, Nigel. You owe me five hundred and three dollars."

Across the river, on the far side of the racing course, a 4.5-metre cedar launch ties up against the boom. The owners raise a portable canvas awning and then lay out a picnic in the shade. We realize, with sudden pangs, that it is time for lunch, and head for the adjoining café. The posted menu informs us that, for the miniscule sum of £28, we can dine upon a half-lobster salad.

"What half of the lobster do you get?" wonders Linda. "The tail or the head? I don't want to pay twenty-eight quid for a salad that might wink at me."

We head back toward the Leander Club on the not unreasonable expectation that if you're going to pay some ludicrous sum for lunch you might as well dine well. By now, the owners of the portable marquees have returned to their cars, and various banquets have been laid out upon the tables. The crowd around the Bentley has a fine spread of *foie gras*, cheeses, fresh bread, and cold cuts. I do a quick calculation based upon what it would cost to host eight people at the restaurants here and realize that, even when you throw in the costs of the food, marquee, and Bentley, you're still ahead.

When we reach the Leander Club, we discover that we should have reserved a place in advance—there are no tables available. We opt for an outdoor pint of Pimm's. It is cold, fizzy, and very refreshing, with a ginger and lemon taste enhanced by fresh mint. While sitting beneath a shady chestnut tree imbibing our drinks, I note that virtually everyone sitting around us is wearing pink socks. *Damn*, these are good drinks.

Since it's obvious we aren't going to get anything here to eat without taking out a mortgage, we leave the grounds and head to Chateau du Vin.

A rather flustered Felix rushes out of the kitchen to kiss me and shake Linda's hand. "*Ooh-la-la*—I have a hundred covers for tonight alone. I'm going to need a vacation after this." We order the cheese and ham omelette, which is excellent, and about one-tenth the price of comparable grub down by the river. We head back, fully sated and all the wiser to the gastronomic ways of the regatta.

There is something about a full belly that stimulates the metaphysical senses. Sitting in the grandstands, the even, methodic rhythm of the competitors as they surge by, the sonorous drawl of the announcer as he calls the progress of each race down the course, the seemingly endless parade of well-dressed people streaming by—you can't help but imagine that all is well with the world. It is all so very, utterly, charmingly English.

That night, Teddy invites us to the Barn Cottage Boat Club Memorial Dinner. When we arrive at the Leander Club at 8 PM, we are escorted upstairs to the main dining room, where Teddy is entertaining a dozen guests.

Chris Davidge, who evidently appears to have overcome his burst blood vessel episode, explains to me that until the mid-1950s the teams from each country that competed in the Olympics were the best clubs, rather than the best rowers.

"We said to each other, we don't care if it's your team or my team, let's just get together," he says. The only way they could do that was to form their own special club and, under the patronage of Teddy, Barn Cottage Rowing Club was born. "And that was the beginning of modern rowing."

The dinner, roast beef and horseradish, is excellently cooked and presented. After the meal, Peter, Teddy's neighbour and long-standing friend, gets up to do the honours. "Teddy's father was a rowing instructor at Cambridge. And do you know why? He was no good as a priest, so they said, 'Let's make him a coach.'" Teddy takes the insults with great relish and everyone ends the evening with a toast to his health.

By the time we leave, the stars have come out. The Angel is doing a booming business at the far end of the bridge, and the pair of burly security guards have a long line of people waiting to get in. Farther down the lane, near Andy's marina, a trio of police squat around a man lying comatose on the sidewalk. "Had a little too much to drink tonight, did we?" asks one copper. We detour around and make our way home.

Thursday dawns to a damp rain, so we decide to give our livers a break and take the day off the regatta and concentrate on house-hold chores. Outside Waitrose, Jackie is standing by her flower stall having a smoke. I ask her how business is going.

"We was busy this morning, lots of folk are entertaining this week."

"Are you going to go down to the regatta?"

Jackie gives a wicked grin. "Are you kidding? It's more fun standing here and watching the crews go by—such a lovely sight."

Waitrose is largely deserted. The few patrons who are there are obviously on their way to the regatta. An elegant woman in a black silk summer dress and sun-hat is purchasing some peaches in the fruit section. A young girl with pink and green crew colours woven in ribbons through her hair is buying fags at the customer service desk.

"It's so boring when it's this empty," says Louise at the express desk. "It just makes the day run so long." She counts out my change, handing me a few coins and a dingy-looking five-pound note.

Why is it that five-pound notes are so much filthier than the rest of Britain's currency? Are you supposed to keep it tucked in your shoe, as opposed to your wallet? Normally I like colourful money, but I am more than a little concerned that the fiver is dyed green in order to conceal as much of the fungal grunge clinging to its exterior as possible. I read in the paper that the Queen never carries cash, which is just as well, because if she ever saw the condition that her portrait is reduced to on a daily basis, she would campaign for the reintroduction of heads on pikes at Tower Bridge.

Friday arrives bright and clear. We head for Teddy's yard, where his friends June and David have set up a marquee and are laying out a picnic spread from the back of their Jaguar coupe. At least, I think they are Teddy's friends. It could just be they are Cambridge alumni from out of town and have asked Teddy if they can use Barn Cottage to hold a reception. Either way, June, who is wearing a very expensive Versace silk suit in leopard skin print and what looks like a knuckle-duster made of solid gold, has a smile that is looking a little brittle as she tries to ascertain exactly how many of the dozen people hovering around the spread have been invited by Teddy and how many are just interlopers.

"Care for a quail's egg?" she asks me.

The orbs in question are rather tiny and speckled and look decidedly fussy, but I decide that it would be best if I just eat one before June punches me with her jewellery. Taking one in hand, I laboriously pick away the thin shell to reveal what, at first glance, looks exactly like a normal egg, only tiny. I dip it in celery salt and pop it into my mouth, where it explodes briefly in wonderful, spicy flavour. No wonder crows go to all that fuss to scavenge them out.

David pops by to refill my glass with more champagne. I suddenly realize that if I were to stack up all the bottles I've helped empty versus the number of races I've seen, it would be a dead heat.

Since it is our first day with badges to the exclusive Steward's Enclosure, we decide to go over and see what the fuss is all about. The main entrance is staffed by six security guards. As we are entering, they have waylaid a young woman, perhaps twenty-one, with a splendid décolletage barely constrained beneath a silk blouse. The problem is not with her exposure up top; it is the fact that an erogenous zone below is seriously exposed. The security man, dressed in black suit and bowler hat, shakes his head. "I'm sorry, Miss, but all ladies have to cover their knees." She protests, but the man stands firm with arms crossed. A compromise is reached by lowering her skirt waistband until the offending region is covered and propriety is served. As she passes into the enclosure, I note with approval that she has a butterfly tattoo on her left cheek. At least, decorum is served.

The enclosure is laid out in a long line of tents housing various cafés, watering holes, and lavatory facilities. We stop at an oyster bar, where, for £60, you can wash down a dozen Brittany #1s with a litre of bubbly. We opt for a pint of Pimm's, which at least comes with its own fruit salad, then find a table and watch the world go by. The world, in this case, consists of an endless procession of finely dressed people attempting to balance four champagne flutes and a plate of bivalves on a bucket of ice. The women hobble majestically about in Charles Jourdan sandals, the high heels digging into the soft turf with each step. It is all very regal, and I could swear I spotted Her Majesty gliding casually through the crowd. *Damn*, these are fine drinks.

The main grandstand is positioned adjacent to the finish line. It features swank seats and an all-weather cover and is reserved for the regatta grandees. I notice several people seriously at slumber, oblivious to everything around them.

A steel railing with attached bar stools has been positioned adjacent to the walkway. It is unreserved, and family and friends of the rowers can stand at this point and offer their support. We mosey up to the bar and blend in.

Since the course is more than a mile long, the regatta has come up with an interesting method of keeping viewers informed. At each main point of the race (essentially the one-quarter, halfway, and three-quarter markers), an official on a barge in the middle of the river posts a marker on a board that indicates who is winning, and by how much. This is very handy, as the announcer tends to carry on in an indecipherable drone.

I hear the contestants approach the finish line before I see them. All along the course, the crowd hollers encouragement as they pass. The roar slowly approaches, until the two boats surge into view. It is a very close race, with less than half a boat length separating the two teams, and their arms and torsos are taut as they pull with all their might for those last few metres. I have absolutely no idea who the two teams are, but I am filled with excitement at the thrilling climax and join in the shouting. The team in purple out-muscles their competitors and cross the line first. They drop their oars into the water and collapse backward, slapping each other on the back in victory.

That evening, after the races, we are enjoying a respite on our home balcony. Jazz music floats across the river from a party being held beneath a copse of chestnut trees. The sweet smell of ribs on the Angel pub's outdoor barbecue floats in the air. Judging from the noise level and activity, there is definitely an air of heightened inebriation in the festivities.

A boat bearing half a dozen young men approaches from upstream. They are dressed in gaily coloured party frocks, complete with wigs, high heels, and lipstick, and they are belting out a lusty rendition of "It's Raining Men, Hallelujah." A rather tipsy woman staggers toward the shoreline and waves her bottle of champagne in the air in encouragement, but is prevented from swimming out to join them by her boyfriend's arm around her waist. A police boat from the Environment Agency is positioned in midstream, but their main concern seems to be keeping the river traffic moving in the right direction, which is just as well, as, by my reckoning, a Breathalyzer checkstop would have confirmed approximately 98 per cent of drivers over the limit; the officers are probably the only sober people for miles around.

It is Saturday morning. Teddy has once again invited us over to Barn Cottage for somebody else's picnic. This time, it is Eton College's party, complete with Scotch eggs, sausage rolls, and Sauvignon Blanc. It is a pleasant change from champagne and quail's eggs. John, a barrister whose wide, cherubic face is complemented by the tiny racing cap jammed on his head, introduces me to Michael something-Flavisham, the Queen's horsemaster. It turns out that Michael has a brother in Vancouver, which is only a thousand kilometres from my hometown, Calgary, and might I know him? Sadly, I don't, but Anne Marie, a young, buxom woman in a huge black-and-white hat, bursts forth nearby with a gale of boisterous laughter for no apparent reason, and we never finish our conversation.

It turns out Anne Marie is the personal assistant to Prince Edward, and insists he is far nicer than what he appears. I consider this rather a backhanded compliment, but she is referring to what the press makes him look like. We ask about the differences between the Henley Regatta and the horseracing Derby at Ascot, which she recently attended.

"I feel much more comfortable here," she notes. "Ascot has really lost its charm. There are loads of people sunning topless in their Rolls and sicking up."

I am about to enquire further, especially about the topless business, when Teddy pops by on his Henley-Davidson and announces that we are on our way to join some old chums from Oxford for lunch. We bid farewell and make our way along a grassy track to the far side of the meadow, where a picnic is being hosted by Christopher and Olivia, old friends of Teddy's from London. The meal is a very pleasant mix of Coronation chicken, saffron rice, and green salad. We finish off the meal with a raspberry and cream Pavlova.

By 3 PM, I have had so much champagne that I am beginning to piss bubbles. We bid adieu to Teddy and his friends and wobble off to, at the very least, see one more race. We arrive at the finish line just in time to catch a heat involving one of the Canadian teams and, by chance, bump into the coach of the Canadian squad. Mike is a native of Marlow who has been coaching the Canadians for more than a decade and has been directly responsible for them winning several Olympic medals. He is a slight, quiet-spoken man, but his skill at coaching is unquestionable. After a few polite words, he excuses himself in order to watch the races. It is a good day for Canada, and all the teams advance.

We return to Boathouse Reach for a rest and enjoy dinner on the balcony. As evening descends, the traffic and noise begin to significantly pick up. The transvestite boat returns, but this time the passengers have doffed their frocks in favour of large balloons that have been tied to their naked loins in a creatively crude manner.

Just after dark, thousands of people begin streaming toward the centre of town. The bridge has been close to car traffic, and the enclosure grounds opened to general traffic. Precisely at 10 PM, the skies over the Thames are lit up by a tremendous display of pyrotechnics. Huge rockets scream skywards, filling the dark sky with bursts of blue, yellow, red, and gold, and rocking the valley for a good fifteen minutes. It finishes with a huge salvo of explosives that blanket the ether with dazzling light before tailing off into darkness. When it is finished, a thick cloud of sulphurous smoke drifts inland, losing itself among the trees like a wraith.

The next morning, we rise late and pack our tummies soundly with a breakfast of bacon, eggs, and toast. Most English epicures make sure things are tamped well down with fried tomatoes, black sausage, and beans, but I didn't dare risk mixing any further combustibles into a region of my body already overloaded with methane.

Instead of heading down to the grounds, we have decided to view the races from a river perspective. At three minutes prior to 2 PM, we make a dash for *The New Orleans*. Even though it is only forty-five metres from our front door, we are almost too late, and Kim is just making ready to cast off as we run up the plank.

"Canada is racing at 3 PM," I explain, clutching our large flag. "Do you think you can find us a spot to cheer them on?"

Kim calculates the boat's course in his head for a moment. "It's a close thing, but I think we can reach the start." I give him the thumbs-up and head for the bar.

The New Orleans is older than *The Hibernia* and, frankly, classier. The main cabin has been done in plush seating and dark panelling, which gives it a nice paddle-wheelie air. The curved bar is well stocked with beer and wine, and they have added a pitcher or two of Pimm's for the occasion. We order our drinks and head upstairs.

The top floor has been furnished with plastic tables and bright red and white umbrellas. I take a moment to observe the guests onboard. The woman to my left in mauve polyester is wondrously large, and her purse is so crammed with cigarettes that she has to hold her two emergency packs in her left hand. An American family to my right is confusing the seagulls with their nasal twang, and a lad in a Newcastle kit is trying to drink two pints of lager simultaneously. Well, definitely not your Steward's Enclosure crowd, then.

Kim swings the massive boat through a U-turn and heads in the direction of the bridge. Since there is so little clearance, we are all ordered downstairs so that the boat can pass underneath without knocking any passengers off. This proves to be an inconvenience to the polyester lady, as she must not only put out her three cigarettes but must also navigate back down the stairs. Kim has to keep the boat neutral in midstream while two of his deck hands manhandle the woman into the main cabin.

From the river, the main grandstand looks, well, grand, and I notice that the farther you are away from the inhabitants, the grander they look, too. A pair of boats come surging up the course, so we pull out our flag and wave it, but it's just two teams from the States, so we tuck it back in. Don't want to waste any good flag-waving vibe on *them*, now do we?

We soon pass the main enclosure and into the first half of the course. This is new, uncharted territory for us, mainly because we'd been too inebriated previously to stagger this distance for a first-hand look. I am immediately impressed by the vitality and tackiness of it all; in addition to an immense sign announcing a hog roast, there is a dual set of inflatable Budweiser bottles towering six metres above the thirsty throngs that crowd the bank. Acre after acre of trailer parks, hospitality suites, shooter bars, and burger stands beckon us as we cruise along. Fawley Court mansion, resplendent in a new coat of sienna paint, looks a little like a debutante having a dirty night out among it all.

We reach the starting point slightly before 3 PM. Kim swings the huge boat around and we drape our flag over the side of the boat. "Go Canada!" we shout, and they do, quickly surging ahead of their American competitors to take the lead. The American family, who had obviously left their flag at home so as not to attract the attention of Al-Qaeda, are envious. We holler our lusty support until the teams are out of sight. From the scoreboard in the distance, however, we can see that our team wins by three lengths. The fat babe celebrates with a *hip-hip hooray* and kisses me on the cheek and pinches my bum. They sure love their regattas around here.

It's been almost two days now since I gulped my last flute of Veuve Clicquot and the strain is beginning to show. I find my lips puckering the moment I hear a French word, and as for the smell of *foie gras*, well, let's just say that drool isn't the sort of fashion statement I want to make on my tuxedo lapels. So it is with great anticipation that we don our fine raiment and head for the Henley Festival of Music & the Arts.

A lot has happened in the last two days. The regatta tents are still there, as well as the flock of geese crapping copiously on the docks, but all else has changed dramatically. An immense bandstand tent has been set up on a thirty-metre-wide barge and towed into place in front of the grandstand. Various metal patchwork sculptures of giant peacocks, dragons, and roosters have been scattered across the wide expanses of lawn. Murals of supernova starbursts have been strung from canvas tents. If the purpose of the art is to scare off small carrion birds from your garden, then most of it is brilliant. I judge the security staff, patrolling the grounds to prevent their theft, a complete waste of money.

The several thousand guests are attired in evening wear, the women in ball gowns and the men in black tie. One or two of the men have opted for vests brocaded in gold and silver, which is tacky enough, but a few have gone right overboard and donned cummerbunds. You might think that a six-inch-wide truss in bright red worn on the outside of the shirt might not be the best way of distracting attention from one's spare tire, but apparently not here. Personally, I think there's a wonderful endorsement opportunity here for Michelin.

We head for the nearest champagne bar, where a female pirate charges us £15 for a half-bottle of bubbly. Sipping on our drinks, we head for the floating stage. A large lawn area between the grandstand and the floating stage, imaginatively referred to as "The Lawn," has been carpeted with a thousand folding chairs. The sea of green is rapidly filling up, but we find comfortable seats with both a view of the stage and the sunset.

This evening, Benjamin Zander is conducting the Royal Philharmonic Orchestra at the main stage. He is a tall, rather charismatic man wearing tails and a large shock of white hair. He exhorts the audience in a thick Teutonic accent to hold onto their bladders for the musical adventure ahead. We prepare for Tchaikovsky's overture to *Romeo and Juliet*, a piece that the Russian composer, Zander assures us, found so exquisite that he shot himself. Thus firmly in the correct frame of mind, we settle back for the show.

The forty-piece orchestra is in fine fettle as they launch into the romantic tragedy with the intensity that only a cadre of world-ranked professional musicians beset by gnats can muster. They sprint through the fight scene between the Montagues and the Capulets and positively dash through the blessing of Friar Laurence to get to the final bloodbath and family lament, *amen*.

Well, no need to worry about the bladder, so far. At this rate, they'll be finished fifteen minutes before they start. The tone of the program changes dramatically, however, as the Oxford Choir stands and bursts forth into a stirring rendition of Mozart's *Ave Verum Corpus*. As the ecclesiastical music floats forth, I lean back into my chair and gaze off into the distance. To the west, the sun is setting behind a lacework of chestnut trees. High overhead, clouds saunter by, their thick aubergine bottoms giving way to golden caps as they capture the last fleeting rays of the sunset. The sky turns a deep cobalt blue, and a flock of geese in V-formation fly upstream to their evening sanctuary. It is heaven.

Zander's last selection for the evening is Beethoven's *Ode to Joy*. Four operatic singers join the orchestra and choir onstage, and the hundred-plus ensemble launches into what many consider the finest choral music ever scored. The force of their passion is so intense that a man who had fallen asleep nearby leaps so violently awake that his chair collapses and he smacks his head open on a steel girder supporting the grandstand. Does it get any better than this?

I am standing outside of the Henley Festival's ladies' toilet, waiting for Linda to exit. The full moon, pale and golden, is rising slowly over the distant chestnut trees. The sound of classical music carries gently from the floating stage. The smell of grilled steak wafts in the breeze. Somewhere out on the Thames, another champagne cork is launched into the air. All around me, women in sparkling ball gowns and men in black tuxedos are talking about the evening's lineup of performers. Everyone, that is, except for a man with a long, sloping forehead, pale blond hair, receding chin, and protruding teeth. He is standing beside me giggling as he zooms the lens of his digital camera in and out.

"What are you doing?"

He points toward the loo. "Don't you see the sign? It says 'Ladies.'" This sets off a guffaw of laughter. A woman in an elegant, sheer silk dress walks past.

"Neville, you are *so* dull. Stop that," she says. Neville, who, at a guess, has about two bottles of bubbly under his sails, ignores her, happily taking snaps of women exiting the facilities until a bout of hiccups momentarily interrupts his activity.

"Are you going to create your own website?" I ask.

"What a marvellous idea! What should I call it?"

"How about Kinky-loo.com?"

"*Ha-ha-ha!* Splendid!"

I have further questions regarding his sanity, but Linda takes me in hand and leads me back toward the stage.

Lesley Garrett is headlining tonight, and the audience eagerly awaits her arrival. She doesn't disappoint, descending from an open vintage touring car dressed in an emerald-green frock. She immediately belts out an Elvis tune, "The Wonder of You," then glides through a wide range of songs, including an aria from *La Boheme*, Paul McCartney's "Blackbird," a Hungarian folk ballad, "Ave Maria," and that one about Bali by Sting.

For many of Lesley's fans, the most enjoyable aspect of the concert is that they can smoke while she performs. About half a dozen audience members seem intent on contracting emphysema before intermission. One woman literally lights one stick off the last, just before it chars the filter. I suspect they have some special attachment at home, a little metal clamp screwed onto the arm of the couch that allows them to eat in front of the telly and switch the remote without having the burden of putting their fags down first in an ashtray.

After the show, we head for the smaller concert marquee. Bob Geldof was supposed to play but, to my great relief, he has been replaced by the Fine Young Cannibals. All the portable seats

have been removed from the open-sided tent so that the audience can dance to the music. By the time we arrive, fans have already begun to crowd in, but we are still able to find a spot some four metres from the stage. The FYC promptly take the stage at 11 PM and launch into one of their big numbers, a cover of Elvis's "Suspicious Minds."

I don't know what kind of audience FYC generally attract but, judging from some of the action, I would have to say exhibitionist fornicators is a good guess. A tall man to my right is taking it in the back porch from what I assume is a close friend, or perhaps an opportunist, as they sway to the music. I assume they're from London, as I have never noticed a tuxedo with a fly down the back at The Men's Shoppe on Bell Street. They disappear after the song, perhaps stepping out for a smoke, since it's not allowed in the tent. They are replaced by a couple who bear an uncanny resemblance to Meat Loaf and Liz Taylor. He is a mountain of a man, all white jacket and man-breasts, while she is tastefully attired in a chiffon dress, purple toreador jacket, and three chins. When the band launches into a slow number, she turns around, hikes up her skirt, and does a bump-and-grinder with her big boy.

With all this love in the air, you'd think the old aggro would be under control, wouldn't you? There's nothing like a little lager to bring out the lout, however. A man in a kilt takes objection to an elbow in his wife's ear as an avid fan tries to push his way to the front. Fists are shaken and words ensue, but you can only get so nasty in a skirt, so things calm down before Angus and Stuart get a right ruck started. We take this as a sign of things to come, and after the band finishes its set we bid adieu to the Henley Festival and beat a retreat back home.

13

AUGUST

Time to Go

It is an absolutely gorgeous English summer afternoon, and I am celebrating it by committing blasphemy. Specifically, I am sipping a pint of ale that I have poured out of a tin can. Just to add insult to injury, I have chilled the can down to a woefully low temperature in the fridge. Worst of all, it is a cream ale, one that comes with a widget that induces an artificial head of foam when opened.

At this point, one might expect the heavens to open and a bolt of lightning to strike me dead, but so far the portents are surprisingly amenable. In addition to its brilliant blue, the afternoon sky is lightly festooned with innocuous fluffy clouds. A gentle zephyr rustles the chestnut trees that line the far shore. Scullers row past the ducks that paddle about in the river, and pedestrians queue patiently to buy cones of soft ice cream from a riverside vendor. I lean back into my balcony lounger, tip my glass to the gods, and take a sip.

Linda appears on the balcony and gives me a kiss. "Hello, you're home early," I say.

"That's because I'm done at work. For good."

I narrowly avoid spraying beer all over her. "What?"

Linda sits down in the lounge chair beside me. "They have a new IT system and they no longer need me. They're not renewing my contract. It's time to go home to Calgary."

I immediately hide my frosty glass under the lounge chair, but it is obviously too late; I have been smote. "But we can't go back, we've just settled in!"

Linda kicks off her shoes. She has been working hard the last year, and she has had enough. I know she yearns for our condo on the shores of the idyllic Bow River, and misses our little cat, China, who is being cared for by friends in our absence. "We can stay as long as you like—all you have to do is get a job."

"You know, I kind of miss Calgary, too."

Linda reaches under my lounger for the beer and takes a sip. "I thought you'd see it my way."

The next morning, I rise bright and early to begin organizing our move. We have relocated from one continent to another several times in the last few years, and I have learned through painful experience that the only way to do it is make a list and check it twice. I write down all the necessary cancellations, notices, and disposals, then grab my coat and head out the door.

I should comment at this point that, even though we have been living here full time for an entire year, I have not met a single American on the streets of Henley. There are lots of them about, I am sure, but they are either using some mysterious cloaking technology developed by the CIA that makes overfed people with loud nasal accents and complex digital cameras completely invisible, or I have been insanely lucky.

Until now, of course. I am standing in line at the Royal Mail outlet while a woman ahead of me purchases stamps. She is perhaps forty, with frizzy blonde hair and wrap-around California sunglasses. She approaches the desk clutching a fistful of postcards in one hand and a purse in the other. "How much does it cost for *You Ass*?" she asks.

The clerk, a heavy-set woman with short dark hair and a lip ring, has the slightly confused look of someone who suspects they've just been propositioned for sexual favours. "I beg your pardon?"

"The States." She waves her correspondence in the air. "How much for a postcard?"

"*Ah*. It costs forty-seven pence per card for airmail service."

"I got ten. How much does that come to?"

The clerk rolls her eyes slightly skyward; perhaps the rates are painted on the ceiling. "That would be four pounds seventy."

The woman places the postcards down on the counter, the better to fish in her purse. It is a large leather accessory with a stylized logo that makes it look like a cheap forgery instead of an expensive designer product costing thousands of dollars. She pulls out numerous articles of personal hygiene until she finds a change purse; after several minutes of closely examining coins in the faint hope of recognition, she finally extracts a £5 note and hands it to the clerk, who dutifully counts out ten stamps and hands back the change.

As she walks by, I point to the stamps. "I hope you're not going to lick those."

"Why not?"

"Cockroaches lay their eggs in the glue. A woman in Surrey cut her lip while licking one and three days later all these maggots burst out." The woman turns very pale and heads for the door. It's a wonderful feeling, doing your civic duty.

After filling out my change of address form at the post office, I head down to the Market Place to cancel the household insurance. Dale the busker is nowhere to be seen or heard, but the flower ladies are busy selling cyclamens, blue cabbage, and other decorative fall plantings from the back of their lorry. "*Oy*, Love," shouts Jackie when she sees me. "Something for the missus?"

"Sorry, I have to pack all the vases away," I reply. "We're moving back to Canada."

"*Ooh*, that's a shame." Jackie takes a small bundle of carnations, places the stems in a plastic bucket, and hands them to me. "There, that's for being such a nice gentleman and buying your wife flowers all the time."

"Thanks, Jackie. That's very sweet."

On the way back, I stop in at Mr. Trowbridge's. Richard is coming over tonight, and I need to pick up some meat for the barbecue. When I tell the butcher that we will be going home soon, he disappears into the back storeroom and returns with a meat pie, a specialty of the establishment. "Here, I wanted you to try this before I put them out. It's a new one."

It smells quite delicious. "What's in it?"

"Canadian back bacon and apple sauce. I hope you like it."

I am walking down the street eating my pie when I pass the Chateau du Vin. A sign in the window says *Closed*, and workmen are busy hoisting tables and chairs out the front door and loading them into a lorry. Felix emerges carrying a box of crêpe pans and a rolling pin. "What happened?" I ask.

"The restaurant, she is, how you say…?"

"Bust?"

Felix blows a raspberry. "Yes, *boost*!"

"Where is Claude?"

"Gone! I am owed a month's wages!"

"I'm sorry to hear that; what will you do now?"

Felix drops the box on the sidewalk in order to properly shrug, that eternal Gallic response to adversity. "I will go back to Toulouse. Perhaps I will open my own restaurant."

I give Felix a big hug. "Thank you for the wonderful meals. I wish you and Rose all the luck in the world."

"*Au revoir*, my friend." He picks up his box of cooking utensils and heads down the sidewalk.

That evening, Richard shows up with several bottles of real ale. "Did you know the Chateau du Vin closed?" I say.

"Doesn't surprise me," says Richard. "I told them a million times to lower their price of beer, but they never listened." We open two bottles of ale, then Richard joins me on the back balcony

overlooking the river while I cook dinner. It consists of chicken thighs mixed in a Portuguese marinade of olive oil, garlic, paprika, oregano, and lemon juice. As the meat cooks, the fat and marinade drip down into the burner, sending up a savoury cloud of smoke that wafts along the marina. Richard points to the boats that churn through the water and the languid shore beyond.

"I suppose this is pretty tame scenery compared to Canada," he says.

"No, it's beautiful," I reply, and I mean it.

That evening, after Richard has gone home, Linda and I take advantage of the warm evening to uncork a bottle of St. Emilion and sit on the upper balcony. A waxing moon is rising in the east, and boats, their pilot lights glowing blue, pass slowly in the river. A night bird calls somewhere, its sweet voice hanging in the warm, humid air.

I think back to what Richard said earlier. There is something that I have grown to love about the gardenlike neatness of the English countryside, the intimacy of it all. It's not as though nature has been tamed—we came close enough to being inundated by a flood to realize that—but it's the delight that British people take in their natural surroundings, a desire to cultivate trees and protect wild species, all with an eye and an appreciation for what it adds to their lives. Beauty comes in all shapes and forms; I shall miss waking in the morning to the honk of swans, mist rising from the river, and rowers sculling through the water.

I phone the movers, and their representative, an Irishman named Liam shows up the following Tuesday. Measuring tape in hand, he patiently scours each room, tabulating every item. I am aware that we've managed to collect a sizable amount of junk over the course of a year, but when he shows us the estimate for shipping everything back to Canada, I am stunned. "This can't be right," I say.

Liam leans over my shoulder and points to the clipboard. "I never in me life seen so many shoes."

Linda takes the clipboard and scans it closely. "Well, I guess that means only one thing—a garage sale."

"What are we going to get rid of?"

Linda glances down through the list. "Golf clubs, garden tools, that rubber skull from Stratford…"

"No shoes?"

Linda looks at me as though I've been eating too much beef and then turns to the mover. "Don't worry, Liam, when you get back next week, we'll have it down by half."

I am put in charge of depleting our household effluvia. It turns out that it's not as difficult as expected; once I factor in the different voltage for the TV, the odd size of the bedsheets, and the fact they won't let you carry dahlia tubers across the border, some progress is made.

Of course, one obstacle remains: how do I arrange a garage sale?

Unlike Canada, where you simply put an ad in the newspaper announcing the date and hopelessly daft people show up at your door at 6 AM Saturday morning, the English have a tradition of rummaging at boot sales. Sadly, *THE BIG ONE* sale isn't for another month. I am mulling over my options while mooching about the kitchen cupboards when I come across a set of wine glasses that Andy loaned me last Christmas. Packing them into a box, I take them around the corner to the marina.

Inside the cramped office, Jack is sitting at the main desk, busy on the computer. He thanks me when I return the wine glasses, then shows me a site that lists boats for sale. "I'm thinking of getting something new," he explains.

I immediately catch the implication. "Congratulations on finally taking the helm. Where's your dad?"

"He's outside, washing down his new car."

I amble down to the end of the marina where Andy is standing with a bucket of soapy water. The vehicle in question is a 1953 Morris Minor convertible, painted pale yellow with a red leather interior. "Wow," I exclaim. "It's beautiful."

Andy beams with pride. "It's the same year as Clare and I got married. I always wanted one."

I stand to one side as Andy splashes about, rubbing the car with a sponge. "So, now that you're retired, what do you intend to do?"

"I've got some old rugby mates in New Zealand I'd like to visit. Clare and I are going to head down there this fall, after the boats are put away."

"I'm surprised you'd ever want to leave; you said yourself Henley is the best place in the world."

Andy gets a gleam in his eye. "Well, I guess it makes it that much easier to come home to, doesn't it?"

A light bulb suddenly goes on. "Speaking of home, you wouldn't happen to need a few previously loved items at reasonable prices, would you?" I dig out my list, upon which I have carefully tabulated all of our old sheets, towels, electric utensils, along with suggested sale prices. Andy scans the list. "Okay, I'll take 'em."

"Which?"

"All of it."

Well, that makes things a tad easier, doesn't it? As I am walking back around the corner feeling very much pleased with the world, someone calls out my name. It is Teddy, sitting in Peter's car. He rolls down the passenger window and beckons me over. "I am having the worst day—my car didn't pass the MOT inspection!"

"What happened to it?"

"Teddy bored it to death," says Peter.

I don't want to make his day any worse, but I know I have to tell him eventually. "Teddy, Linda is finished her work here. We're heading back to Canada soon."

Teddy's eyes go round in astonishment. "What? Don't be ridiculous. You belong here."

"We'd love to stay, but we can't." A horn honks; Peter's car is blocking traffic. The car pulls out and they disappear down the lane. I feel badly, as though I've disappointed Teddy. I promise myself to visit him the next day.

The following day is uncharacteristically brilliant, and the locals don't like it one bit. Shoppers scurry across the pavement to the shelter of shady awnings, casting scowls at me as I blithely mosey along in the noonday sun.

The lane leading to Barn Cottage is shaded by an immense hedgerow, and were it not for parched drivers barrelling desperately along the road toward the Flower Pot Inn for a pint of cooling ale, I would have the world all to myself. I reach the meadow adjacent to Teddy's home; except for the occasional upended champagne bottle peeking above the grass, there is nary a sign of the recent shenanigans. Teddy is at home, relaxing in the cool shade of his sitting room, and invites me in. Sitting in an ancient stuffed chair, he has doffed his traditional vest and soup-stained trousers for a sleeveless undershirt and khaki shorts. "Didn't happen to bring any brandy, did you?"

"Sorry," I reply. "How about a nice cold glass of water?"

"Have to do, I suppose. Help yourself in the kitchen."

It's the first time I've really had a chance to look at Teddy's home. It's a farmer's cottage, one-and-a-half storeys, with a dining room in addition to the sitting room and kitchen. A narrow stairway winds upstairs to the bedroom and single bath. The kitchen itself contains little more than a stove, ceramic sink, some cupboards, and a large table for canning vegetables; the rough stone floor is scuffed by generations of workboots and the baseboards chewed by puppies long since gone. I find two glasses and turn on the tap; the water is fresh, cold, and clear.

By the time I return, Teddy has found an old regatta catalogue and is using it as a fan to stir up a breeze. I hand him his water and then do a visual tour of the sitting room, which is crammed with books, worn-out riding gear, the official Barn Cottage Boat Club flag, and not a few empty bottles. I am especially interested in the photos, most in black and white, the few colour pictures faded and curled. They catalogue not only Teddy's life, but his ancestors' as well, images dating back into the nineteenth century, the subjects standing rigid in their formal wear of bowler hats and long, sweeping dresses. Teddy points to one photo on the bookshelf. "That's my grandfather, the Bishop of New Zealand."

"You mean the one wearing the grass skirt?"

"*Haw-haw.* That's the one. There's a college at Cambridge named after us, you know."

I point to a photo of a beautiful horse. "Who's this?"

"Moonee River. My wife Pamela's. She knew how to spend money, that one."

"Still around?"

"She's just up the road, in the Remenham Cemetery. Last I heard, she hadn't gone anywhere."

I laugh. "Linda and I are going to miss you, Teddy." I turn back to the photos; there is one of my host, resplendent in his RAF uniform. "What do you think ever happened to that girl you met after the war?"

"Anne? I got a letter from her a few years ago. She came to visit me at the Leander Club." Teddy smiles slightly. "You know, I might just look her up. You never know."

We talk of this and that, me laughing at Teddy's various misadventures, he cursing his sore hip. I promise to write when we are back in Calgary, and he promises to call. I leave him, still fluttering his catalogue, surrounded by a lifetime of triumphs and tragedies, memories and ghosts.

The day before we are to leave, the movers arrive, load up our remaining possessions, and cart them away. That evening, Alan and Niina take us to their favourite restaurant, Antico's, nestled behind the town hall. The dining place is run by Valerio, a handsome and charming man from northern Italy. He conducts us to a table near the leaded windows overlooking the street; we are settled in amid a collection of ancient pots and pans and musical instruments that clutter the walls.

Niina orders roast chicken and fresh spinach cooked in butter and garlic; Linda and I opt for the pan-fried shrimp in herbs, and Alan orders the white fish poached in wine sauce. It is all delightfully good, especially when washed down with several bottles of Chianti. All small talk desists as our ears disappear below the lips of our bowls.

Finally, over tiramisu and coffee, conversation resumes. "Now that you're successful as an artist, what do you intend to do?" I ask Alan. "Are you going to launch a new career as a painter?"

"We're going to travel and see the world first, then decide," says Alan. "I'm just filled with such a positive feeling these days."

Valerio joins us with a complimentary bottle of wine, and we all toast each others' futures. It is very late when we finally stagger out into the night; the sky is filled with a million hazy stars, due, no doubt, to the evening mist.

The following morning, the hired car arrives to take us to the airport. The driver loads our bags into the back, and we close the door to our home for the final time. Alan and Niina come out and hug us and wish us a safe journey, then wave as we drive off.

The chauffeur circles through the centre of town past St. Mary's Church and then crosses the river. I throw a careless salute out the window to Colonel Bogey as he marches across the bridge. As we head up White Hill toward the M3, I crane my neck to glance back one last time. On my right is the Leander Club, and in the distance, Barn Cottage. On my left is the Angel pub and the stretch of river leading back to Boathouse Reach.

I set out to write about the Toffs and snobs and inbred Twits of Henley, but aside from that ninny Simon the publisher, I didn't really encounter any. We were welcomed with open arms by Teddy and treated with the greatest respect as Canadians by our landlord Andy. Our neighbours Alan and Niina turned out to be lovely people who we will keep as friends for the rest of our lives.

In the end, I was wrong; the people of England truly *are* warm and charming.

Drat.

Epilogue

As might be expected, little has changed in Henley-on-Thames since our stay there. Traffic still snarls at the drop of a snow-flake, merchants still gripe at paying £50 for scrawny Christmas trees, and copious amounts of champagne are still consumed each year at the Henley Royal Regatta.

As for our friends, Teddy has passed away, and now rests in the St. Nicholas church graveyard adjacent to his beloved Regatta course. Alan has temporarily forsaken his paintbrush to invent new electronic gizmos, and Richard has been promoted to managing editor of the *Henley Standard*, which means he can make everyone else use the wretched digital camera. Valerio makes the best Italian food in town, and the flower girls will gladly admire any male's well-shaped derriere.

And the Thames flows ever on—placid, immutable, and steeped in tales.

Acknowledgements

I wish to thank the people of Henley-on-Thames for being so wonderfully eccentric, and for welcoming Linda and myself with kindness and generosity of spirit. I especially wish to thank Teddy Selwyn, Richard Reed, and Alan and Niina Buckett.

This book would not be possible without the enthusiasm and support of all the folks at RMB, including Don Gorman, Chyla Cardinal, Joe Wilderson, and Neil Wedin. I would also like to thank Charlene Dobmeier and Meaghan Craven at Fifth House.